NATIONAL GEOGRAPHIC
Prehistoric
Mammals

Created and produced by Firecrest Books Ltd.

First U.S. edition published by the National Geographic Society
1145 17th Street N.W.
Washington, D.C. 20036-4688
U.S.A.

Library of Congress Cataloging-in-Publication Data

Turner, Alan, 1947-
  National Geographic prehistoric mammals / by Alan Turner;
illustrated by Mauricio Antón.
      p. cm.
  Includes index.
  Trade Edition ISBN 0-7922-7134-3
Library Edition ISBN 0-7922-6997-7
  1. Mammals, Fossil. I. Title.
  QE881.T87 2004
  569—dc22
                                    2004001189

Printed in China

NATIONAL GEOGRAPHIC
Prehistoric
Mammals

ALAN TURNER
ILLUSTRATED BY MAURICIO ANTÓN

NATIONAL GEOGRAPHIC

Washington, D.C.

Acknowledgments

Thanks are due to Miguel Carrascal for
helping to initiate and coordinate the project.

The publishers also wish to thank the following for permission
to reproduce the pictures used in this book:

The Natural History Museum, London:
10, 11 (top), 31 (top), 33 (top right),
36, 45, 46, 54, 57, 63, 67, 75, 81, 84,
88, 90, 94 (left), 94 (right), 96, 100,
117, 134, 136, 162, 164, 184, 101;
Dave Watts: 11 (bottom);
C. Campbell: 26, 49, 51;
Mauricio Antón: 27 (top left), 27 (top right),
31 (bottom), 60, 62, 68, 71, 87, 103, 112,
120, 130, 142, 156, 170, 180, 181;
The Zoological Society of London: 48;
Carnegie Museum of Natural History, Pittsburgh: 58;
The Field Museum, Neg # GEO78432: 168;
University of California Museum of Paleontology: 179

Additional artwork by
Israel Sánchez:
pages 24-25, 42-43, 45, 46-47 (bottom left), 50-51,
54-55, 58, 60-61 (right), 84, 102-103 (right), 104,
118, 134-135, 137 (top), 138-139, 150-151,
162-163, 164-165, 168-169, 184-185

and Martin Camm:
33 (top left), 39 (pangolin, flying lemur, taeniodont,
pantodont, hyrax, monotreme, rabbit)

Note on the art: The artists used pencil and oil paint on layers of
translucent paper and on canvas to achieve the various effects you see
throughout the book. They began working with the most recent
skeletal information on each animal, then built the tissue layer before
adding the final details of fur or skin.

Color separation in Singapore by
SC (Sang Choy) International Pte. Ltd.

Published by the National Geographic Society

John M. Fahey, Jr., *President and Chief Executive Officer*
Gilbert M. Grosvenor, *Chairman of the Board*
Nina D. Hoffman, *Executive Vice President, President of Books and
Education Publishing Group*
Ericka Markman, *Senior Vice President, President of Children's Books and
Education Publishing Group*

Staff for This Book
Nancy Laties Feresten, *Vice President, Editor-in-Chief of Children's Books*
Jennifer Emmett *and* Marfé Ferguson Delano, *Project Editors*
Bea Jackson, *Art Director, Children's Books*
Michelle R. Harris, *Researcher*
Judith Klein, *Copy Editor*
Connie D. Binder, *Indexer*
R. Gary Colbert, *Production Director*
Vincent P. Ryan, *Manufacturing Manager*

Prepared for the National Geographic Society by
Firecrest Books Ltd.

Peter Sackett, *Publishing Consultant*

Norman Barrett, *Editorial Director*

Joyce Pope, *Contributing Editor*

Phil Jacobs, *Designer*

Pat Jacobs, *Project Coordinator*

Contents

Introduction

When we look around today, we see a world teeming with mammals. There are lots of them and lots of different kinds—some 5,000 living species. Mammals flourish in a wide array of environments, some of which are hostile to life of any sort. Their evolutionary story is one of some success. Beyond sheer number of species, mammals are adapted to extraordinarily different lifestyles, and they vary profoundly in size and appearance. Body weights range from less than a sixth of an ounce (5 g) for some shrews and bats to more than 180 tons for the blue whale. Mammals can and do live in trees and some can hang from their tails; some are proficient diggers and live underground. Some are capable of powered flight, and still others never leave the water. But this diversity of living species is just the tip of the iceberg. The present represents a single, relatively small, slice of time in a mammalian pedigree that extends back about 220 million years. Fully two-thirds of mammalian history took place during the Age of Dinosaurs, when the landscape was dominated by those ruling reptiles. Mammals of this time period were generally small and presumably did not occupy a very broad range of ecological niches. It became an entirely different story after the terminal Cretaceous extinctions, 65 million years ago, when mammals underwent an explosive evolutionary expansion. Most of the modern groups appeared by about 55 million years ago, and mammals have been a conspicuous part of terrestrial life ever since.

This diversity of mammals through the ages is of itself important. Among other things, by tracking the numbers and kinds of species through time, we can develop a broader understanding of the evolutionary process and how communities change through time. But prehistoric mammals also challenge us to understand physical adaptation to the environment and why animals are

8

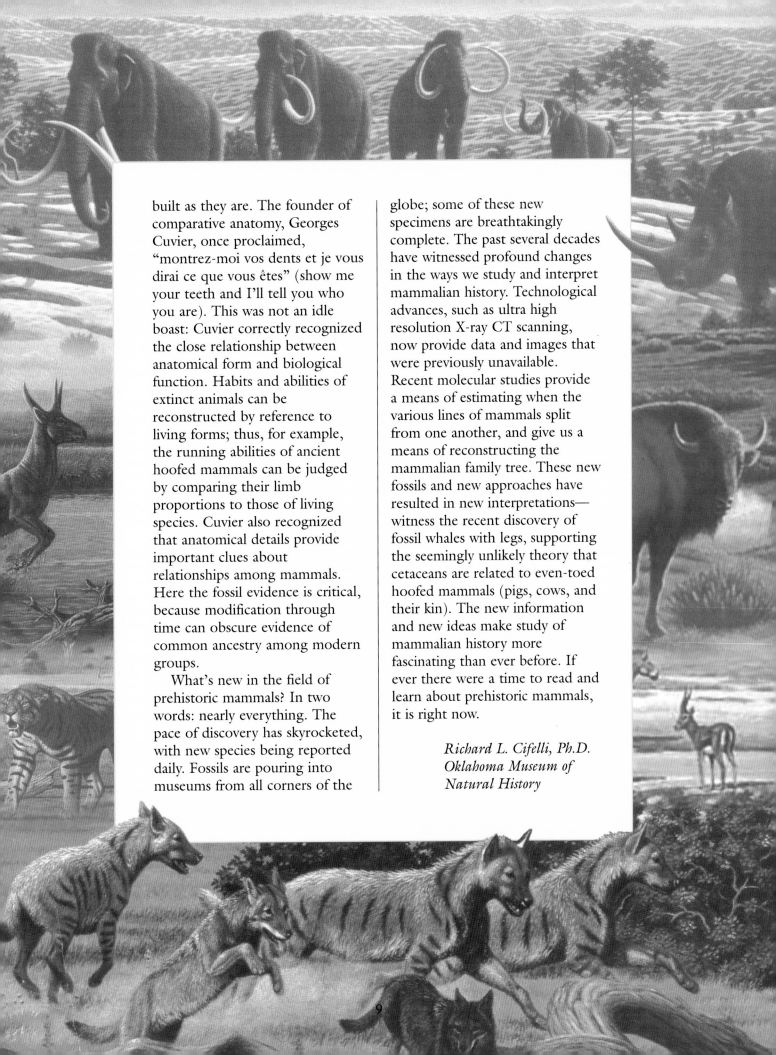

built as they are. The founder of comparative anatomy, Georges Cuvier, once proclaimed, "montrez-moi vos dents et je vous dirai ce que vous êtes" (show me your teeth and I'll tell you who you are). This was not an idle boast: Cuvier correctly recognized the close relationship between anatomical form and biological function. Habits and abilities of extinct animals can be reconstructed by reference to living forms; thus, for example, the running abilities of ancient hoofed mammals can be judged by comparing their limb proportions to those of living species. Cuvier also recognized that anatomical details provide important clues about relationships among mammals. Here the fossil evidence is critical, because modification through time can obscure evidence of common ancestry among modern groups.

What's new in the field of prehistoric mammals? In two words: nearly everything. The pace of discovery has skyrocketed, with new species being reported daily. Fossils are pouring into museums from all corners of the globe; some of these new specimens are breathtakingly complete. The past several decades have witnessed profound changes in the ways we study and interpret mammalian history. Technological advances, such as ultra high resolution X-ray CT scanning, now provide data and images that were previously unavailable. Recent molecular studies provide a means of estimating when the various lines of mammals split from one another, and give us a means of reconstructing the mammalian family tree. These new fossils and new approaches have resulted in new interpretations— witness the recent discovery of fossil whales with legs, supporting the seemingly unlikely theory that cetaceans are related to even-toed hoofed mammals (pigs, cows, and their kin). The new information and new ideas make study of mammalian history more fascinating than ever before. If ever there were a time to read and learn about prehistoric mammals, it is right now.

Richard L. Cifelli, Ph.D.
Oklahoma Museum of
Natural History

9

What is a mammal?

Mammals are warm-blooded, air-breathing animals with backbones and fur or hair, and they feed their young milk. But not all of these defining features show up on fossils.

We are mammals, and so are our close relatives the chimpanzees and gorillas. So also are dogs and hamsters, antelopes and elephants, bats and whales. What is it that links such different creatures that allows us to group them all as mammals? To begin with, all have a backbone composed of vertebrae. But so do fishes and frogs, reptiles and birds. Mammals are air-breathing and warm-blooded—like birds. But mammals do one thing that birds do not—they feed their young milk. The name of the gland that produces the milk is the mammary gland, and it is

this that gives the whole great group, of 4,500 to 5,000 living species and thousands upon thousands of extinct species, its name.

Living mammals may be divided into three groups according to how the young are born. The placentals, which include humans, are by far the largest group. In placentals, the young are protected in the uterus of the mother during a gestation period, and nourished from their mother's bloodstream via a special organ called the placenta. The second largest group is the marsupials, which are born alive after a very short gestation. Once born, the tiny, blind creature must make its way to a pouch on its mother's belly. Here it finds a milk supply by attaching itself to a nipple, and so continues its development. Only a few species of the third group, the monotremes, still exist. They include the duck-billed platypus. Monotremes are like reptiles in some ways—for example, they lay eggs. But they are hairy, and when hatched the young feed on milk, something only mammals do.

Warm-blooded animals have a constant high temperature at which their body works best. As a result, they are ready for action at any moment. This is not so for reptiles, for example, which are cold-blooded and have to rely on the sun's warmth for their energy. Mammals, almost all

Below: *The kangaroo is a marsupial mammal. The young continue their development after birth inside their mother's pouch.*

of which can control their temperature, can live in cold or hot climates, and be active in both. Activity depends on fuel—that is, food—being burned. So mammals have efficient systems for gathering and digesting food. To make use of the food, oxygen is needed. So mammals breathe regularly to keep their energy turnover going at a proper rate. But, if possible, energy must be conserved. So mammals insulate their bodies with hair, fur, or fat. Because of this, it is usually easy to tell at a glance that a creature is a mammal—you do not have to find a mother suckling her baby.

Fossil mammals

Unfortunately, hair and fat are hardly ever preserved. When dealing with fossil mammals we have to look at what skeletons can tell us. Teeth, which contain enamel, the hardest mammal tissue, are often the best preserved. Their shape shows us the sort of food that an animal ate. The marks left on the limb bones by muscle attachments tell us whether we are dealing with a creature capable of running fast.

Among the mammal-like reptiles and the earliest mammals, there is evidence of increasing activity. Along with this came an increase in brain size. It is possible that hair developed at an early date. For example, *Thrinaxodon*, a cynodont or "near mammal," had little pits in the bones of its snout, like those of present-day mammals with big whiskers (which are just large hairs). Since we cannot tell when milk feeding first began, we need a further test to distinguish the early mammals from the mammal-like reptiles. This is outlined on pages 44-45.

Below: *Bats are the only mammals capable of true flight. Like elephants and whales, they are placental mammals, which nourish their young in the womb before giving birth.*

Below: *The duck-billed platypus is a monotreme. It lives in water and lays eggs. But the young then proceed to suckle on their mother's milk.*

Age of Mammals

We call the past 65 million years the Age of Mammals. The dinosaurs ruled the Earth for 150 million years, but after they died out the mammals became the dominant creatures of our planet.

A few reptiles and amphibians survived the great extinction of 65 million years ago. But they had had their day, and the mammals and the birds were the ones with the world at their feet. For a time, and in some places, the competition between them for living space and food was great. But eventually the mammals came to dominate the land.

The earliest known mammals

Remains of mammals from rocks 215-195 million years old in China, South Africa, and Europe show us shrew-like creatures about 6 inches (15 cm) long. The teeth are divided into groups with different functions so that they can nip, tear, and slice or chew food. This is made easier because the jaws are hinged like those of modern mammals, and the mouth is altered to allow these animals to chew and breathe at the same time. This results in an efficient digestive system that can extract energy quickly from food. Throughout the Mesozoic era (248-65 mya), a complex range of small mammals evolved, belonging to about two dozen different families. They were almost certainly furry, and probably many of them laid eggs.

When the dinosaurs became extinct, the mammals that had lived

Map below: *The Earth at the beginning of the Age of Mammals, 65 mya. India had not yet moved into Asia, and Australia was still attached to Antarctica. North America was attached to Eurasia but not to South America.*

Bottom: *The Cenozoic era, or Age of Mammals, is divided into epochs, the current one being the Holocene, dating from 10,000 years ago.*

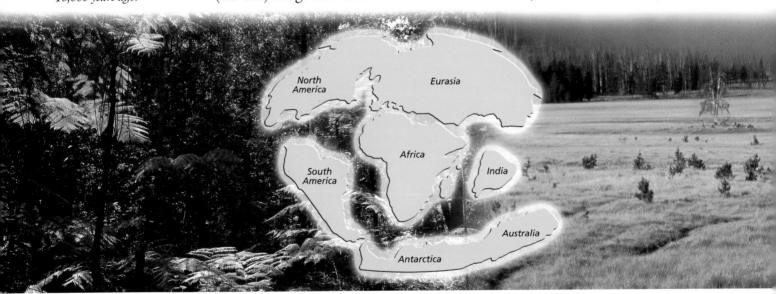

North America

Eurasia

Africa

South America

India

Antarctica

Australia

Paleocene	Eocene	
65 mya	55 mya	34 mya

TERTIARY PERIOD

about their feet for so long found themselves in a world with different plants and no great rivals for space. Rapidly, geologically speaking, they evolved into many forms with differing ways of life. This took place against a backdrop of global change, with continents drifting, high mountains being built, and alterations in habitat that had a great effect on all living things during the past 65 million years—the Cenozoic era, or Age of Mammals.

The Earth's crust consists of rigid, moving plates. These have been responsible over millions of years for the movement of continents. About 220 million years ago the continents had all been joined into one great land mass called Pangaea. This split up during the Age of Dinosaurs, and in the Cenozoic there were further great rifts. The continents began to take their present shape and positions. The African plate crashed into Eurasia (Europe and Asia), shaping the Mediterranean Sea. The Indian subcontinent pushed into Asia,

forming the great Himalayas. Other collisions formed chains of mountains running from western Asia to the Alps and Pyrenees. At about the same time, high mountains were appearing down the west side of the Americas, running through into Antarctica and New Zealand. A little over 3 million years ago, North and South America joined across the narrow land bridge of Central America, while Australia moved northward.

Mammals take over

These great global upheavals caused dramatic changes in climate, habitats, and the distribution of vegetation. But the mammals flourished in the challenging circumstances. As things changed, and some species that were specialized to certain habitats became extinct, others evolved to take their place. This happened fairly rapidly. No living mammal species was present as little as 5 million years ago. But the ancestors of today's mammals can in some cases be identified, including our own forebears.

Map below: *The Earth 10,000 years ago. A different view of the world at the end of the last ice age shows that there was still a land bridge between North America and Eurasia. Lower sea levels meant that North and South America were also linked.*

Below far left: *Rain forests, now largely confined to parts of the tropical regions, were more extensive in the past. Then climatic change—and later human activities— caused them to disappear.*

Below center: *Open grasslands began to appear in the Miocene, a time when grazing species such as horses and cud-chewing mammals started to increase in numbers and spread across the continents.*

Below right: *Mixed grass and woodland such as this was the typical natural vegetation of much of Europe, Asia, and North and South America from the Miocene onward. It contained many plants that would be familiar to us today.*

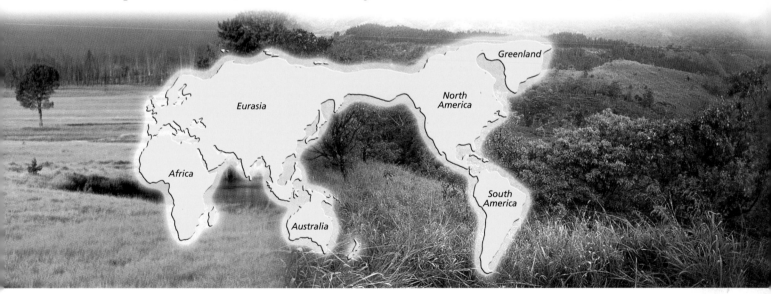

Greenland

North America

Eurasia

Africa

Australia

South America

Oligocene		Miocene		Pliocene	Pleistocene	Holocene
	24 mya			5 mya	1.8 mya	10,000 ya

Uintatherium, massive herbivores with bizarre bony protuberances on their heads, browse a North American forest. The small foxlike predator Sinopa, a member of the extinct order Creodonta, scampers by

Indricotherium, a hornless rhino, is the largest known land mammal. Males reached 20 feet (6 m) at shoulder height. They dwarfed the Hyaenodon, wolf-size creodonts that were the largest predators of the period in Eurasia.

Miocene

The swampy forests of the Miocene were home to Deinotherium, *early elephant-like animals that survived into the Pleistocene. Sharing this habitat were the horse Architherium and, in the foreground, the mongoose Herpestes.*

The rich South American fauna of the Pliocene included the saber-toothed marsupial cat Thylacosmilus atrox (right), the placental glyptodonts (left, a dead one in the foreground), and gigantic ground sloths (background).

Kenya 1.6 million years ago: A small foraging group of Homo erectus attempt to drive a dirk-toothed cat (Megantereon) from the freshly killed carcass of a waterbuck

Other creatures of the Cenozoic era

Although the dinosaurs were gone, the mammals of the Cenozoic were by no means alone on the planet.

By the end of the Cretaceous period, 65 million years ago, the dinosaurs had died out. So had the large, predatory sea reptiles such as the ichthyosaurs and plesiosaurs. The mammals rose to dominance in the Cenozoic era, which followed. But many other creatures that had shared the planet with the dinosaurs also survived, and flourished along with the mammals.

Below: *The Miocene relatives of the living great white sharks, such as this* Carcharodon, *rivaled a killer whale in size.*

Giant sharks, for example, continued to inhabit the seas. Their teeth

Below: *At 20 ft (6 m) in length, and outweighing any competitor among the marsupial predators of Australia, the giant monitor lizard* Megalania *had no enemies and enjoyed its choice of prey.*

have been found by the thousands in some fossil deposits. They were relatives of the living great white sharks of *Jaws* fame, but larger by far than anything portrayed by Hollywood filmmakers. And before the ice ages of the past two and a half million years set in, the earlier part of the Pliocene period was one of

considerable warmth. Crocodiles lived in what is now southern Spain, and giant turtles inhabited the Roussillon region of southern France, where remains of *Cheirogaster perpiniana* suggest an animal up to 6 feet (2 m) in length.

Twenty-foot lizards

On land, huge reptiles lived. Many people are familiar with Komodo dragons, the large monitor lizards presented as a modern horror story. They are feared not only for their size, but also because of the lethal bite produced by bacteria in their saliva. Living dragons from Komodo and some other islands in the

Indonesian archipelago may measure 10 feet (3 m) in length and weigh 330 pounds (150 kg). But these were dwarfed by the 20-foot (6 m) giant *Megalania priscus,* which inhabited Australia and islands to the north during the Pleistocene epoch. This animal might have weighed in at a ton (1,000 kg). Since living Komodos are active and aggressive hunters capable of taking prey the size of a water buffalo, it is reasonable to assume that no Australian marsupial would have been safe from the Komodo's giant ancestor.

Giant birds

In Europe, North and South America, Madagascar, and New

Below: *The giant tortoise Cheirogaster would have presented an interesting although fruitless challenge to a predator like the saber-toothed cat Dinofelis.*

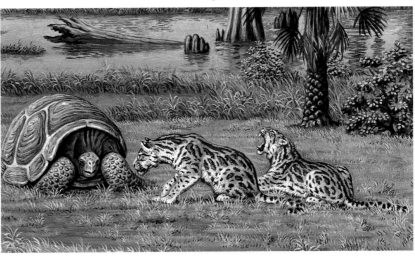

Zealand, the descendants of the dinosaurs—the birds—reached sizes much larger and heavier than today's ostrich. Some were obvious predators, with huge claws and enormous,

Below: *The gigantic predatory bird Andalgalornis had a beak capable of delivering a crushing, fatal bite to almost anything it chose to hunt.*

crushing beaks. And, although the giant predatory birds died out early in the Cenozoic in most parts of the world, in South America—perhaps because it was isolated—they remained a major force. *Andalgalornis* was one such bird, up to 10 feet (3 m) in height and with a skull almost 20 inches (50 cm) in length. It was presumably a fast-moving predator, able to kill either by slashing with its claws or simply crushing and ripping with its beak. When North and South America rejoined across the Panama Isthmus about 3 million years ago, species spread out as far as Florida. But the interchange of animals between the continents seems generally to have led to the final extinction of the giant birds, along with other South American animals, including mammals (see page 56).

Mammal deposits

Finding and recovering mammal fossils is a highly skilled undertaking. It calls for experienced teams of excavators to work in often remote places under difficult conditions.

Below: *The Victoria Fossil Cave, in Australia, is an example of a "bone bed." This is a mass accumulation of bones in one place that provides paleontologists with countless years of excavation work. This bed, one of the richest deposits of Pleistocene fossils in the world, accumulated between 200,000 and 500,000 years ago. It is some 14 ft (4 m) deep and covers an area of about 750 sq ft (70 sq m). Among the 100 or so species represented here are marsupials and placental mammals as well as reptiles, birds, and amphibians, with remains ranging from skulls to complete skeletons.*

Fossils are the remains or evidence of animals or plants that lived thousands to millions of years ago. They range from skeletons to footprints. Fossil mammals are known from all continents, although the records in some parts of the world are better than in others.

Ending up as a fossil is an unlikely fate for any individual of any species. Most leave no trace of their existence after death. To become a fossil, a plant or an animal has to die in the right place so that predators and scavengers are not able to destroy the remains. Even if it avoids that, an animal must be covered in deposits before decay sets in and reduces the skeleton to dust. Those deposits must continue to form after its death. And some process must result in their eventual removal so that the fossil remains can be found.

Recovering remains

For mammals, the most likely place to become a fossil is perhaps a cave, or a stream or lake bed where water can bring more material in to cover the carcass without destroying it completely. To be of use to the paleontologist, those deposits must preserve the remains sufficiently for them to be recognized and identified—usually by study of bones and teeth. Exposure of deposits and fossils may occur naturally with erosion, or wearing away. Or it could happen as a result of human activity such as construction work or mining. In some cases, discovery is the result of a planned search or dig.

Fossils are usually fragile. So, once uncovered, they must be extracted with care. The best way to achieve this is by what is known as a "controlled excavation." This involves a clear recording system, with plans and photographs, showing the relationship between items found in the ground. In this way, individuals can later be recognized and reassembled. Some specimens, such as complete or partially complete skeletons and skulls, may need special

Left: *A typical dig, with paleontologists and technicians working as a team to find, excavate, and record fossils at an established fossil site.*

Right: *Small fossils, such as this skull (viewed from above) of an early form of skunk, can be prepared to a large extent on the spot. The bone visible in the photo had been carefully exposed with tools such as screwdrivers and needles, and bathed at intervals in special solutions to strengthen it.*

Below: *This is how Paracuellos, a valley of the Madrid basin in central Spain, might have looked in the Miocene epoch. During the summer rains, the hillsides would have been eroded. Mudflows would have converged in the valley bottom—dragging and burying the remains of dead animals in the process. Each year, new layers would have formed, giving rise to the successive fossil deposits found there today.*

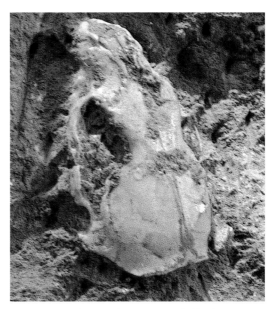

attention from the most skilled workers. These and especially large and heavy items, which will still be fragile, may even have to be removed in a block complete with deposit. They must then be transported, usually to a museum laboratory, where further work will be required to extract them from the material they were buried in.

Reconstructions from fossils

Several teams of scientists work on fossils—extracting, repairing, and reconstructing them.

Below: *Three stages of the reconstruction for an extinct three-toed horse of the genus* Hippotherium *are shown, working from the skeleton to the living appearance. Many of the characteristics of an animal are seen in the way it moves, whether it be an antelope fleeing predators or a cheetah chasing prey. When it comes to reconstructing movement, many general principles from the study of living relatives may be applied. Or, where the fossil form has no known descendants, similarly shaped animals are used as a guide. Here the artist shows* Hippotherium *moving in a manner similar to that of a living horse.*

The first work at the museum may involve extracting the fossils from rock using drills or even weak acids. Broken items must be repaired and fragile specimens consolidated, or strengthened. The individual bones are kept separate until they can be numbered to show where they belong.

Then the task of putting individual animals back together and identifying them begins. This work is carried out by people skilled in recognizing skeletal parts. It involves examining the fossils against a comparative collection. This might consist of other, previously identified fossils or prepared skeletons of living animals. Only when everything has been sorted, mended, consolidated, and identified, does the study of what has been recovered begin.

Building up the image

Reconstruction of extinct animals is built up almost entirely from bones and teeth. Soft tissues such as muscle and skin, or impressions of them, rarely survive. Details like the color and patterning of the coat decay before fossilization. In addition, skeletons are not often complete.

A scientifically accurate reconstruction of an extinct animal's appearance in life must be based on evidence from the skeleton. This provides a clear guide for the position and bulk of the muscles. Only once those muscles have been put in place can the external features be added.

Stages of reconstruction (from left)

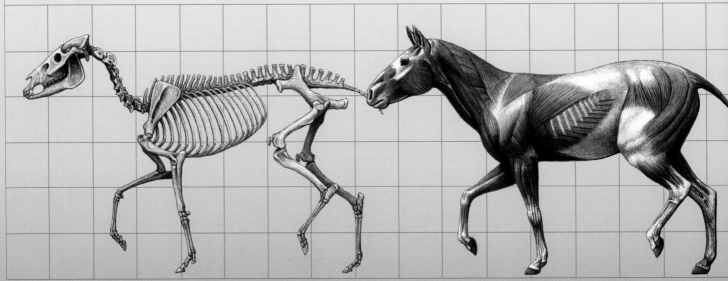

Skeleton

Muscles

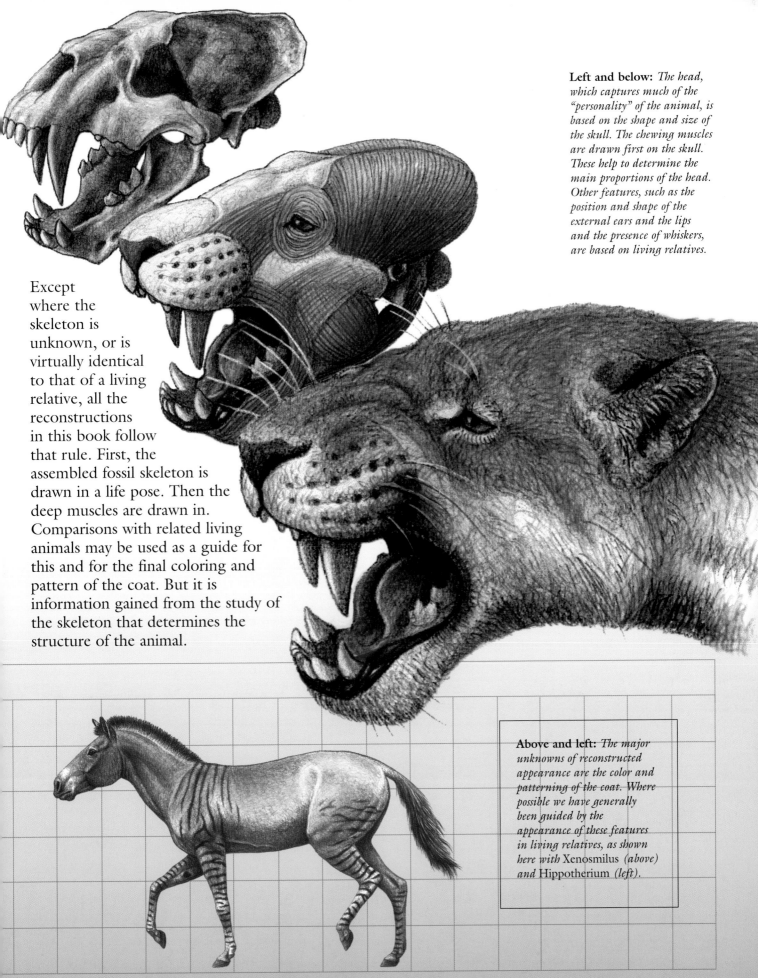

Except where the skeleton is unknown, or is virtually identical to that of a living relative, all the reconstructions in this book follow that rule. First, the assembled fossil skeleton is drawn in a life pose. Then the deep muscles are drawn in. Comparisons with related living animals may be used as a guide for this and for the final coloring and pattern of the coat. But it is information gained from the study of the skeleton that determines the structure of the animal.

Above and left: *The major unknowns of reconstructed appearance are the color and patterning of the coat. Where possible we have generally been guided by the appearance of these features in living relatives, as shown here with* Xenosmilus *(above) and* Hippotherium *(left).*

Reconstruction

How we know

Most of what we know about the behavior of prehistoric mammals has been gleaned from studies of their bones and teeth. In rare cases, footprints or frozen or mummified remains have provided more information.

Below: *The artist's impression of a saber-toothed cat known as* Megantereon cultridens, *identified as such by the bones. We know that modern large cats, such as lions, can spend 18 hours a day sleeping or resting, so it is reasonable to depict it in such a pose.*

Studies of prehistoric mammals are generally restricted to bones and teeth, the only parts that survive in normal circumstances. Fortunately, bones and teeth are still able to tell us a great deal. The skeleton is as much a part of the animal as the muscles, skin, and hair. It is formed through mineralization of tissue made by cells, just like any other portion of the body.

The form of the skeleton tells us what kind of animal it was, and whether it belonged to an order or a family that includes living species. We can also determine how large the animal was, where the muscles were attached and how large they were, how the animal moved, whether it was adult or juvenile, and, in many cases, whether it was male or female.

In rare instances, frozen or naturally mummified remains provide a direct insight into details of the soft

tissues. Perhaps the best known of these are the spectacular finds of mammoths, and other species such as bison and horses, from the permafrost of northern Russia. Permafrost is where the ground has frozen to a great depth and remained frozen for thousand of years—since the animals roamed there. Recovery of complete or even partially complete carcasses is rare, because discovery does not depend just on the thawing of deposits—such as on a riverbank during the short northern summer. It also depends on the chance presence of people in the vicinity who can report the remains. Even then, recovery requires rapid reaction by skilled specialists, who might have to travel huge distances to reach a body before decay sets in and reduces it to a mass of bones and rotten flesh.

Telltale footprints

One other source of information comes in the form of footprints. Although exceedingly rare, these can provide us with important insights into how animals moved. The

photograph below shows some footprints of the extinct cat *Pseudaelurus*. The details of the feet and the pattern of their placement match well with what we have learned about the animal's movement from studies of its skeleton. In addition, the fact that four animals left parallel tracks at the site tells us something about social grouping in the species.

Above: *A baby mammoth, known as Dima ("little girl"), was found in permafrost in Siberia in 1977. She was 6-8 months old at death, an age when living elephants are closely supervised by their mother. This suggests she might have wandered from the herd and gotten stuck in a bog.*

Below: *Fossil footprints from Miocene-age deposits in northern Spain.*

What they ate

"We are what we eat," it is said. Fossil teeth and bones provide clues to the foods prehistoric mammals ate. These clues in turn help experts to reconstruct a mammal's way of life.

Looking at what animals of the past ate helps us to interpret their way of life. Their diet can tell us, for example, whether particular species were forest dwellers or plain dwellers. The teeth of most mammals contain a substance called enamel. It is far harder than bone, so it tends to survive the harsh process of fossilization. Often the teeth are the best preserved part of a fossil

Below: *A* Chalicotherium *browses on the lower branches of a tree in a Miocene forest. The scene has been reconstructed with evidence from fossils of teeth and skeletons.*

mammal. Mammals need to eat a great deal to fuel their high turnover of energy, and have teeth suited to their particular diets. Most mammals may be described as carnivores (flesh-eaters), insectivores (insect-eaters), or herbivores (plant-eaters). But whatever they eat, their teeth—particularly those in the back of their jaws—provide a clue to their diet. In addition, related mammals tend to have teeth of a similar pattern, so we can often place a fossil in its group based on a single tooth.

Clues from teeth and bones

The shape of a mammal's skeleton tells us a great deal about how it lived—whether it was slow-moving or speedy, for example, or a swimmer or digger. The illustration on the left shows a chalicothere eating leaves. We know it did this from the shape of its low-crowned teeth and from its long, hook-clawed forelimbs, which could have been used for little else but pulling branches down to its mouth. Another example is provided by the illustration on page 35. This has been built up from skeletons and teeth that identify the animals as members of the hyena family. But they are more lightly built than modern hyenas, and their teeth are smaller. This tells us that they were probably active hunters rather than scavengers. And they might have hunted in packs, so

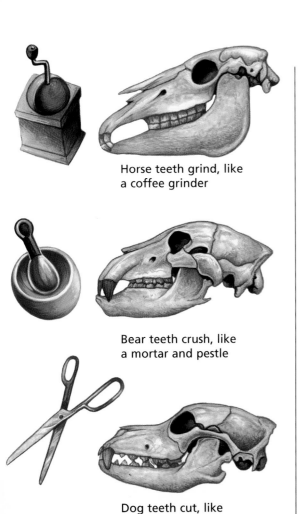

Horse teeth grind, like
a coffee grinder

Bear teeth crush, like
a mortar and pestle

Dog teeth cut, like
a pair of scissors

competition over the remains of a kill was quite possible.

When we look at the whole range of fossil mammals, we can see how their diet and their ways of life changed over millions of years. Sometimes this reflects great changes in the environment, as when horses developed high-crowned, open-rooted teeth suitable for eating grass rather than the leaves of trees. This occurred at a time when grassy plains were becoming commonplace in the world.

"We are what we eat"

The food that we and all other mammals eat forms part of our bodies. So the chemicals that make that food become part of us. Some of these remain unchanged, even in fossil bones. Nowadays we can identify particular chemicals that tell us, for example, whether creatures alive millions of years ago were plant-eaters or meat-eaters.

Above: *This is a coprolite, or preserved dung, of the ground sloth* Mylodon darwinii *from 13,000-year-old cave deposits in Chile. Such rare remains may contain seeds and plant pieces— important clues to diet.*

Left: *The teeth of mammals perform functions similar to a number of human implements.*

Below: *A series of jaws show some of the major differences in the kinds of teeth to be found in mammals that eat a range of foods (human), or specialize in grass (sheep) or in meat (lion).*

Lower jaws, or mandibles, of a human, a sheep, and a lion (not drawn to scale)

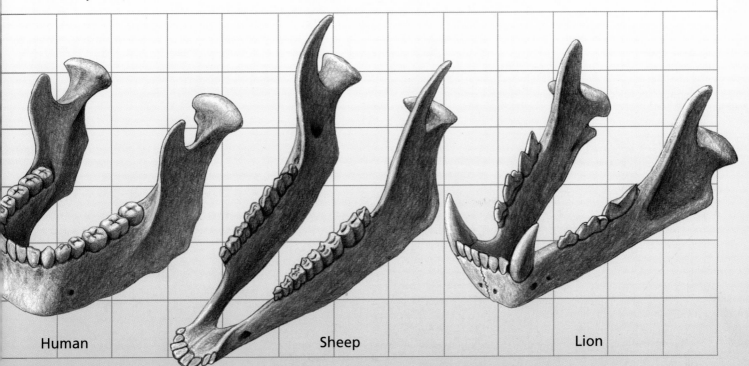

Human

Sheep

Lion

Social behavior

Much of what we interpret as social behavior in prehistoric mammals is based on how living relatives behave. Without this guidance, deductions can still be made from a fossil's features.

Below: *This scene depicts two examples of how teeth might have played a part in social behavior. A pair of male* Anancus *(mastodons) engage in a bout of pushing and shoving with their tusks to establish their status. In the foreground, a saber-toothed* Machairodus *displays his canines, perhaps to reinforce his existing status.*

It is seldom easy to build up a picture of how extinct species behaved socially. We can look at the behavior of close relatives where they exist, but many fossil species have no suitable parallels among those we know today. So we have to base our theories on the evidence of the fossils themselves. We can then make some general points from what we know about mammals with similar features in the living world to guide our reconstructions.

Body features

In living animals we can see that certain body features—whether simply size and shape or ornaments such as horns and antlers—have a function in social interactions between members of a species. Even teeth may be employed, as in

signaling threat or perhaps status. Fortunately, many such features fossilize extremely well. So they can provide us with an insight into social behavior in animals long extinct.

The enlarged canines of saber-toothed cats were undoubtedly deployed in dealing with prey carcasses. They were probably used to bite into a relatively soft area such as the throat once the prey was held immobile. Sinking them into the neck during a leaping attack would have risked breakage. However, part of the evolutionary process that lay behind the development of such teeth might also have had to do with displays to rivals. We see this in lions and leopards today, where a snarl can quickly deter an aggressor before violence becomes necessary. This is not confined to carnivores. Baboon males, for example, also have large canines, and, although they can use them very effectively in warding off attacks from leopards, they also flash those teeth at male rivals.

Establishing status

The tusks of extinct proboscids, like those of living elephants, were simply modified incisor teeth. One of their functions in living elephants is when males use them during bouts of pushing and shoving to compete for access to females in order to mate. In precisely the same way, antelope and deer species use their horns and antlers to establish their status in the herd. So it is reasonable to suggest that extinct mammals such as arsinoitheres—with no living relations—used their horns for the same purpose.

Below: *A pair of hunting hyenas of the genus* Chasmaporthetes *engage in a tussle for the possession of a carcass. In such circumstances, even the most regulated social behavior may break down into a fight for access to food. Suitable-size bite marks resulting from such conflicts might be found on the remains of a prey animal. But even in their absence we could generally predict such behavior from what we know of mammals that operate in hunting groups today.*

Classification

All mammals, like other living things, have scientific names. But whereas most living mammals are known by common names, scientific names are used to describe most fossil mammals.

Zoologists classify mammals along with the rest of the natural world. Fossil mammals can be fitted into the same pattern as the living species.

Scientific classification

Most classification is based on anatomical details, particularly of the skeleton and teeth—the parts most often fossilized. The classification of animals is reflected in their scientific names. Until about 250 years ago, anybody discovering a new animal named it in any way they pleased, and the result was chaos. Then a Swedish naturalist, Carolus Linnaeus, devised a way of classifying plants and animals based on their structure. The scheme, which is still employed today, uses words derived from Latin and ancient Greek, and works in simple steps. An individual is a member of a species, a group of individuals looking much alike and capable of breeding together in the wild. Species are grouped into genera (singular, genus). Genera include species that are closely related, but rarely interbreed in the wild. For example, lions and leopards belong to the same genus but don't breed with each other. Genera are gathered into families, the members of which are clearly related. Families are placed in orders, in which members usually share very ancient common ancestors,

Below: *The lion is classified as* Panthera leo *in any language.*

CLASSIFICATION OF THE LION

Kingdom	Animalia (all animals)
Phylum	Chordata (animals with a stiffening rod, usually a backbone composed of vertebrae)
Class	Mammalia, or mammals (milk-producing, warm-blooded, hairy animals)
Order	Carnivora, or carnivores (flesh-eaters, with some special features, including the carnassials, which are shearing teeth in the back of the jaw)
Family	Felidae, or felids (cats, carnivores with short faces, large eyes, and generally retractile claws)
Genus	*Panthera* (the great cats—distinguished from the small cats by the bones of the throat, which enable them to roar but to purr only as they breathe out)
Species	*leo* (the lion)

so the animals themselves need not look much alike. Orders are put into classes, and classes into phyla (singular phylum), which both contain animals with only the most basic similarities and remote ancestors. The phyla are part of the animal kingdom, which includes all living creatures.

An example is given on page 36 of a classification using Linnaeus's scheme. There are many intermediate groupings, such as suborders or superfamilies, that may be useful in some groups, but these are the main ones. All creatures may be recognized by their two-word scientific classification of genus and species, which is the same in any language and is usually printed in italic type. The animal we know by its common name lion is *Panthera leo*. The tiger, leopard, and jaguar also belong to this genus, but there is only one species of *Panthera* with the name *leo*. The genus always begins with a capital letter. The species always begins with a lower case (small) letter, even if it is based on a proper name. Other levels of classification also have scientific names, such as the cat family Felidae (with a capital), commonly known as the felids, and the order Carnivora (carnivores).

Classifying fossil mammals

The beauty of the system for paleontologists is that it can include fossil as well as living forms. In this way, for example, the orders of mammals that are now extinct can be slotted seamlessly into the pattern. Some of these, such as astrapotheres and pyrotheres, appear to have evolved early in the Tertiary period, but not to have been able to keep up with the great geographical and ecological changes taking place. So they became extinct, leaving no

descendants. But just as we can see relationships between living mammals, the fossils sometimes show us the ancestors from which the present-day forms have evolved. For instance, the condylarths (see pages 132-3) were probably the most ancient ancestors of horses and their relatives, as well as of recently extinct litopterns and *Toxodon*-like animals. This is shown by details of their teeth, feet, and thigh bones, which are similar, but different from all other creatures.

Below: *The extinct North American cat* Miracinonyx inexpectatus, *like the modern-day lion, is a member of the cat family Felidae.*

Mammal groupings

The illustrated diagram on the opposite page depicts the major orders of mammals—those of today as well as ones that have become extinct. It also shows when the extinct orders died out.

Opposite page: *A pictorial representation of the major orders of mammals, showing how they evolved from the Mesozoic era or later, and in which period those no longer with us became extinct. All of the orders in the outer circle have members living today, except for the two marked extinct. The marsupials are treated here as a single order for simplicity, but some scientists believe they should be split into three or more separate orders.*

Below: *A Mesozoic scene depicts multituberculates among carcasses of the dinosaur* Triceratops. *Insignificant as they might appear, these tiny primitive mammals were members of a group that survived for more than 100 million years. The multituberculates looked like rodents, but were not closely related to them or to any other groups of mammals.*

One way of grouping mammals past and present is to divide them into three great subclasses. The chief of these, called the Theria, includes the two major groups of living mammals, the marsupials and the placentals, and their fossil relatives, as well as some fossil forms. The second subclass, the Allotheria, includes creatures that are known only as fossils, most of them very ancient and incomplete. One group of these, the multituberculates, is the longest surviving of all mammal orders. It lasted more than 100 million years, until it became extinct over 30 million years ago. The third subclass, the Prototheria, includes the egg-laying monotremes, only a few of which survive today.

Modern mammals may be divided into some 20 orders. Some of these are very small, such as the aardvarks with only one species. The largest order is the rodents with more than 1,600. Today, the vast majority of mammals are placentals, and, as we can tell from the structure of their skeletons and teeth, so were most of the mammals that lived during the Cenozoic era. The diagram opposite shows the major orders, both surviving and extinct, and the periods from which evidence of their existence has been found.

There is no one answer to the question, "Why do animals become extinct?" Sometimes species or even large orders become closely specialized to a particular way of life. Widespread climatic and vegetation change can happen too quickly for them to adjust. But one of the greatest causes of extinction is thought to be the evolution of more efficient competitors for living space. Should a competitor invade the habitat, or a new species evolve that uses the resources more efficiently, then the animals that lived there will not be able to compete and will eventually become extinct.

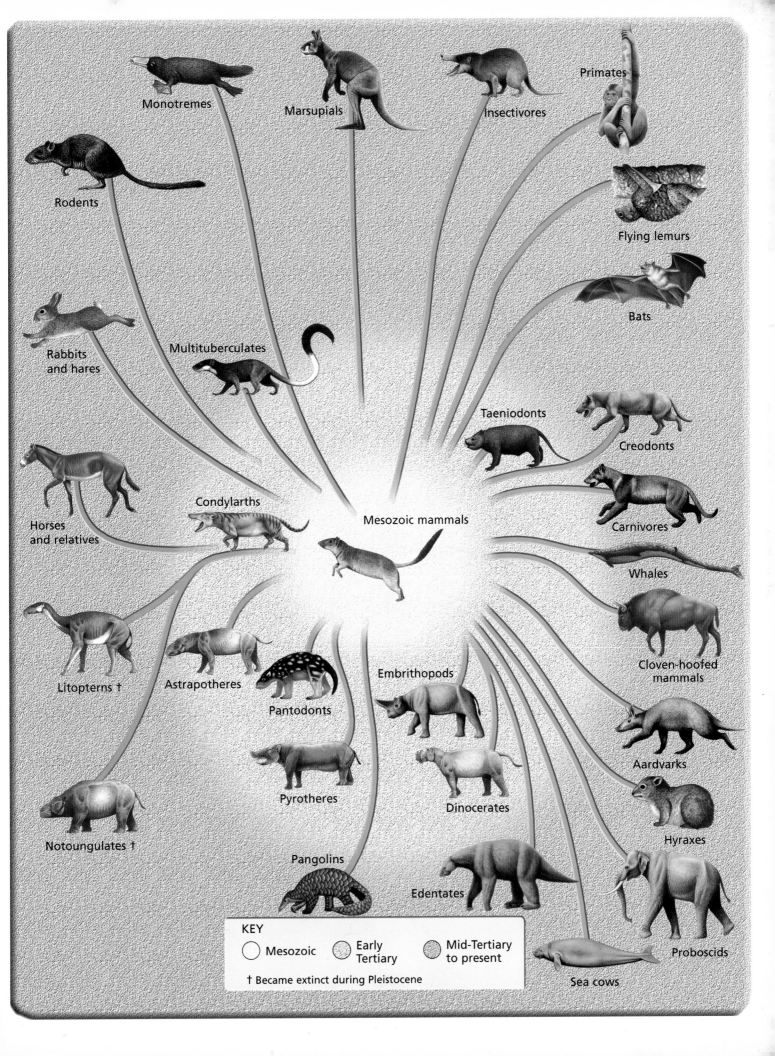

Monotremes

Marsupials

Insectivores

Primates

Rodents

Flying lemurs

Bats

Rabbits
and hares

Multituberculates

Taeniodonts

Creodonts

Horses
and relatives

Condylarths

Mesozoic mammals

Carnivores

Whales

Litopterns †

Astrapotheres

Pantodonts

Embrithopods

Cloven-hoofed
mammals

Pyrotheres

Dinocerates

Aardvarks

Notoungulates †

Hyraxes

Pangolins

Edentates

Proboscids

Sea cows

KEY

○ Mesozoic   ◐ Early
Tertiary   ● Mid-Tertiary
to present

† Became extinct during Pleistocene

Prehistoric profiles

Detailed information about the prehistoric mammals is presented in a series of individual profiles on the following pages (42-187). The features of the profiles are illustrated and explained here.

Most of today's mammals are small. In size, human beings come within the top 5 percent. Mammals may be running animals, or they may hop or swim or even fly—the bats, with about 1,000 species, make up about a fifth of their numbers. Prehistoric mammals came in even more varied shapes, many of which may strike us as bizarre. Because large bones survive the processes of fossilization better than small ones, there are probably many tiny creatures of the past that we shall never know. Equally, there are certainly fossil mammals waiting to be discovered. Even so, from what has been found, we know that the heyday of the mammals came during the Miocene epoch (24-5 mya). Since then, many groups have dwindled and become extinct.

This book presents information about prehistoric mammals in a series of more than 100 profiles. These offer a brief description of the animal and a summarized treatment of the most important facts and figures about it. In most cases, the profiles relate to a species (but sometimes a genus), such as the two South American marsupials shown on the opposite page, *Thylacosmilus atrox* and *Borhyaena tuberata*. The use of Latin names is necessary because although most living mammals have common names that we can use in everyday conversation, extinct species rarely do. An added advantage of using the formal scientific names is that they define an animal precisely in any language.

Each profile is accompanied by a reconstruction of the mammal, a fact file, a size comparison, and a time band. There are sometimes other illustrations relating to the mammal and a map showing where in the world its remains have been found. These features are explained opposite in the captions.

Section heading

Profile, or brief
description, of
the mammal

Introductory summary

Silhouette of a modern-
day *Homo sapiens* for
size comparison

Table giving scientific
name, dimensions, and
date and place details

The name or names of
the species (as here) or
just the genus relating
to the time bands

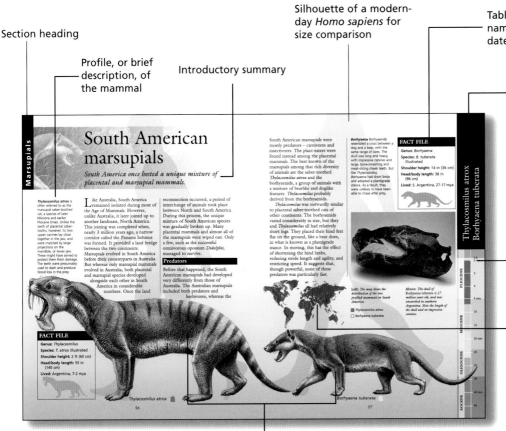

The colored bands indicate the
estimated period of time during
which the species (or genus) existed.
Scientific methods used for dating
finds are constantly being improved.
But the farther back in time you go
or the fewer finds there are, the less
confidence there can be in the
accuracy of this estimate.

Map showing where in the world
remains of the mammal have been
found. It is beyond the scope of this
book to pinpoint all the finds of a
particular species, and maps should
be treated as instant visual guides to
the general region or regions where
it is believed the species lived. It
must be remembered also that,
when many of the profiled species
were alive, the world was a very
different place from what it is now.

Scientifically reconstructed painting of the
mammal based on evidence ranging from
complete skeletons to a few bones and perhaps
the appearance and behavior of living relatives

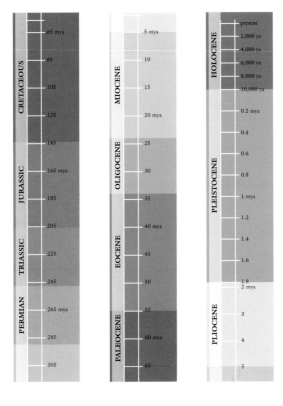

Left: *Three main time bars
are used in the profiles. The
first (far left) covers the
period from the Permian to
the end of the Cretaceous in
steps of 20 million years. The
center bar runs on from the
Cretaceous to cover the period
from the Paleocene to the end
of the Miocene in steps of
5 my. The last bar runs
through the Pliocene in steps
of 1 my, the Pleistocene in
steps of 0.2 my (200,000
years), and then the Holocene
to the present day in 2,000-
year steps.*

Right: *A silhouette of a
6-foot (1.83-m) modern-day
Homo sapiens, drawn to the
same scale, appears next to
the reconstructions. In the
case of smaller mammals,
only part of the silhouette
may be shown.*

Mammal-like reptiles

During the Permian period some reptiles began to develop mammal-like features.

Inostrancevia alexandri was a big gorgonopsian, about the size of a grizzly bear. Its remains have been found in late Permian rocks, which date back about 250 million years. Its limbs were tucked partly under the body, so it stood clear of the ground, much like a mammal. And it could probably run fairly fast, at least for a short distance. It had big claws that would have helped it capture its prey. The huge upper canine teeth were probably not strong enough to stab a victim to death, but might have been used for tearing chunks of flesh from the carcass. These would have been swallowed whole, for it had no strong chewing teeth in the back of its mouth.

Most early reptiles had thick, heavy legs that sprawled out from the sides of their bodies. They were slow-moving and clumsy, and probably spent most of their time resting. But some species belonging to a group called the therapsids developed longer and more slender limbs. These were modified to hold the body clear of the ground and to move it forward easily. They could move more readily over rough terrain, either in pursuit of prey or to escape predators.

Some of the early members of the therapsids, such as the gorgonopsians, must have been fearful hunters. At the front of their jaws they were armed with menacing

teeth, and behind these lay huge saberlike canines. Yet the teeth in the back of their mouth, where the power for chewing or slicing food lies, were small and inefficient. This indicates that these creatures still had a reptilian way of life, with a low turnover of energy. Other mammal-like reptiles that existed at the same time were more progressive. The reptilelike, single-cusped teeth changed to a pattern with three cusps and three roots—the forerunners of the complex teeth of typical mammals.

Mass extinction

A great mass extinction of life took place at the end of the

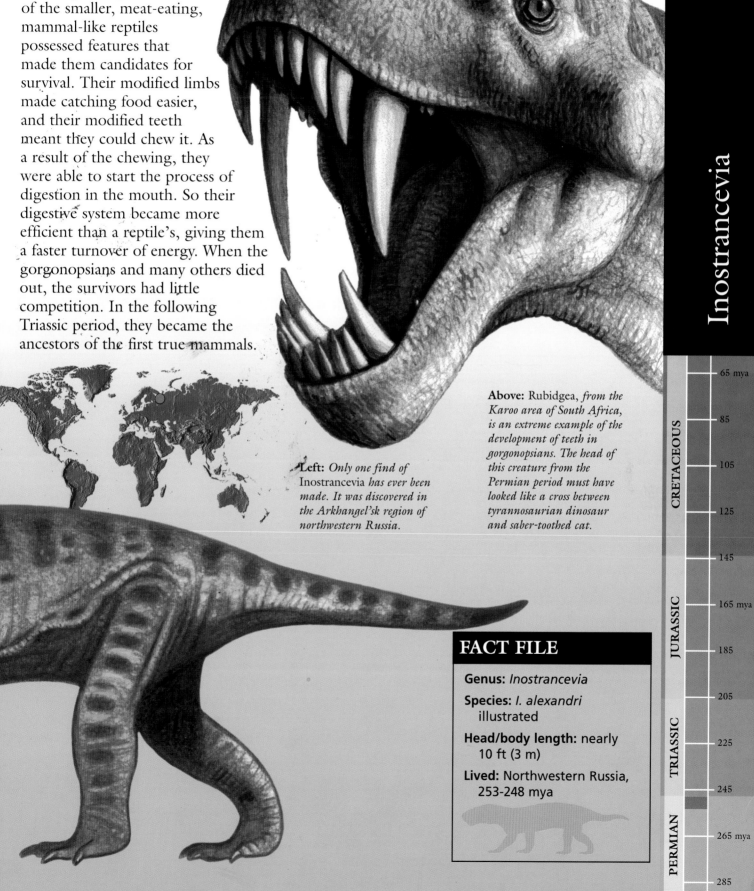

Permian period, about 250 million years ago. But some of the smaller, meat-eating, mammal-like reptiles possessed features that made them candidates for survival. Their modified limbs made catching food easier, and their modified teeth meant they could chew it. As a result of the chewing, they were able to start the process of digestion in the mouth. So their digestive system became more efficient than a reptile's, giving them a faster turnover of energy. When the gorgonopsians and many others died out, the survivors had little competition. In the following Triassic period, they became the ancestors of the first true mammals.

Left: *Only one find of Inostrancevia has ever been made. It was discovered in the Arkhangel'sk region of northwestern Russia.*

Above: Rubidgea, *from the Karoo area of South Africa, is an extreme example of the development of teeth in gorgonopsians. The head of this creature from the Permian period must have looked like a cross between tyrannosaurian dinosaur and saber-toothed cat.*

FACT FILE

Genus: *Inostrancevia*

Species: *I. alexandri* illustrated

Head/body length: nearly 10 ft (3 m)

Lived: Northwestern Russia, 253-248 mya

Inostrancevia

	65 mya
CRETACEOUS	85
	105
	125
	145
JURASSIC	165 mya
	185
	205
TRIASSIC	225
	245
PERMIAN	265 mya
	285
	305

Cynodonts—"near mammals"

A group of mammal-like reptiles called the cynodonts were the direct ancestors of today's mammals.

Among the survivors of the great Permian extinction (see pages 42-3) were members of a group of reptiles called therapsids. Some therapsids, such as the gorgonopsians, died out. But the cynodonts, which survived, included the direct ancestors of today's mammals. Fossil evidence reveals many changes that made the cynodonts more efficient. For example, a plate of bone developed across the top of the mouth and separated the air they breathed from the food they chewed—so they could eat and breathe at the same time, as we can. Changes in the shape of the ribs suggest they developed a diaphragm, which made regular breathing easier. We cannot tell from the fossils whether these animals

Kannemeyeria belongs to a very successful group of plant-eating reptiles, called dicynodonts, that lived in late Permian and early Triassic times. Slow moving, with little obvious means of defense, *Kannemeyeria* might have fallen prey to cynodonts such as species of *Cynognathus*.

suckled their young. But it is likely that they were partially warm-blooded, and fossil footprints indicate they had a covering of hair.

Reptile or mammal?

So where do we draw the line between fossil reptiles and the first mammals? It has to be an arbitrary decision, and experts have chosen a feature that changed very late in the development of mammals. This concerns the way they chewed their food. Reptiles, which hardly chew their food, have a lower jaw that uses a special small bone—called the articular—to hinge it onto the back of the skull. As the mammal-like reptiles began to chew their food more thoroughly, they developed a

Kannemeyeria

44

knob on the main tooth-bearing part of the lower jaw—the dentary bone. This knob rocked against a different part of the skull, making the articular bone and one other small bone in the reptile jaw redundant. These little bones were not lost, but, strangely, they shifted into the skull to become part of the hearing apparatus of mammals. Mammals have three bones

in each ear and one jawbone. Reptiles have three bones on each side of the jaw and only one little bone in each inner ear. And that's how we distinguish between fossil reptiles and fossil mammals.

Cynognathus is a genus of cynodonts from early Triassic rocks in South Africa. The genus contains many species of different sizes, but they are typified by a tiny articular bone as part of the lower jaw, so they are classified with the reptiles. *Cynognathus* was a flesh-eater, and rather doglike in appearance, although it was more heavily built with a skull up to 16 in (40 cm) in length. Its teeth are in many ways like those of mammals, but it could not chew.

Left: *The skull of* Cynognathus *shows perfectly the derivation of the name, which means "dog-jawed," since the overall appearance is indeed similar to a dog.*

Cynognathus

CRETACEOUS

65 mya
85
105
125
145

JURASSIC

165 mya
185
205
225

TRIASSIC

245

PERMIAN

265 mya
285
305

Mesozoic mammals

The earliest true mammals that coexisted with the dinosaurs were small and seemingly insignificant creatures. But they included the ancestors of all living mammals.

Right: *This skull, from Lesotho in Africa, is more than 200 million years old. It belongs to the shrewlike* Megazostrodon, *one of the earliest mammals known.*

Vincelestes neuquenianus is known only from nine individuals from the lower Cretaceous La Amarga Formation of Neuquén Province in Argentina. It suggests what an ancestral therian mammal—the ancestor of both marsupials and placentals—might have looked like. Features of its upper and lower teeth indicate progress toward the complex interlocking teeth of advanced mammals—an adaptation that allows more efficient processing of food.

The Mesozoic era (248 to 65 mya) is known as the Age of Dinosaurs, and the mammals that coexisted with them were

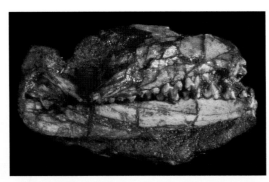

insignificant creatures. Yet they were the ancestors of all living mammals—monotremes, marsupials, and placentals. Their size suggests that they probably existed largely on a diet of insects, a nutritious and abundant

source of food. But we shall probably never know the true extent of their lifestyles or relationships because the fossil record is limited—the bones of tiny animals are fragile and less likely to survive after death to become fossilized. One thing is more certain, however, from recent fossil finds. These tend to confirm the idea that the marsupials and placentals are more closely related to each other than to the monotremes.

"Rodents of the Mesozoic"

Among the oddest of the Mesozoic mammals were the multituberculates, one of the most successful of all known mammal groups. They enjoyed an evolutionary history of more than 100 million years,

FACT FILE

Genus: *Vincelestes*

Species: *V. neuquenianus*

Head/body length: 11.5 in (29 cm)

Lived: Argentina, 140-130 mya

Vincelestes neuquenianus

until they became extinct during the Oligocene. The name multituberculate reflects the fact that the animals' cheek teeth had numerous tubercules, or cusps, apparently used for grinding food. But their large incisors gave them the appearance of rodents, and they have been called the "rodents of the Mesozoic." The range of features in the group suggests lifestyles in the trees and on the ground. They do not sit easily within any of the living groups of mammals except perhaps the monotremes, the primitive group to which the platypus belongs.

Nemegtbaatar gobiensis is a late Cretaceous multituberculate from the Gobi Desert in Asia. It is known from more complete skeletal remains than most of the group. The skeleton suggests it had a jumping style of movement on the ground, as do many small mammals. In overall appearance it would probably have been a rather gerbil-like animal.

Below left *The map shows the known distributions of the two profiled Mesozoic mammals.*

FACT FILE

Genus: *Nemegtbaatar*

Species: *N. gobiensis* illustrated

Head/body length: 7 in (18 cm)

Lived: Mongolia, 70-65 mya

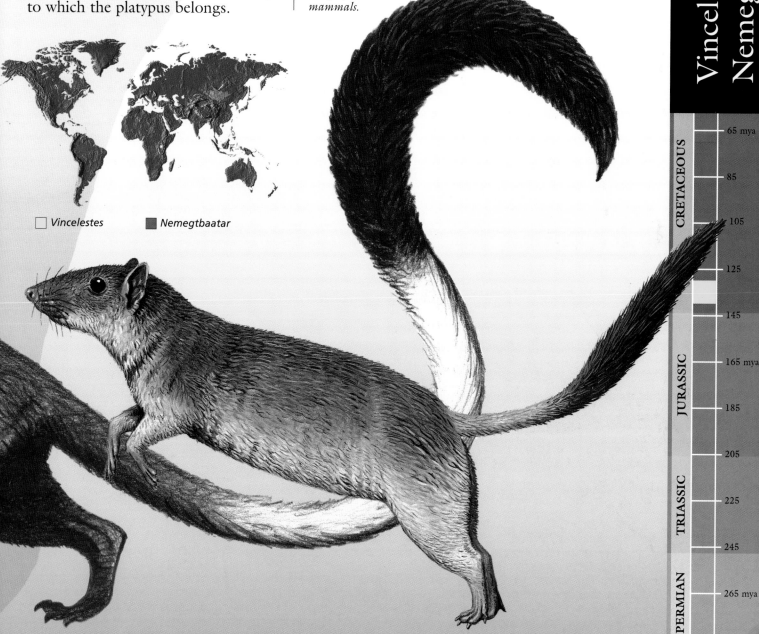

☐ *Vincelestes*   ■ *Nemegtbaatar*

CRETACEOUS — 65 mya
— 85
— 105
— 125
JURASSIC — 145
— 165 mya
— 185
— 205
TRIASSIC — 225
— 245
PERMIAN — 265 mya
— 285
— 305

Marsupials

Australian marsupials are noted not only for their variety compared with the South American ones, but also for the huge size of some extinct species.

Above: Thylacinus, *commonly known as the marsupial (or Tasmanian) wolf, was the largest of the recent marsupial carnivores. It reached weights of more than 66 lb (30 kg). The specimen in the London Zoo (above) was filmed during the 1930s. Fossils have been found throughout Australia and in some islands to the north, but it was restricted to Tasmania before it became extinct.*

Today marsupials, or pouched mammals, are found mainly in Australia, with a small number in New Guinea and the Americas. But the fossil record of marsupials in South America suggests that they were once a significant group of animals among the mammals of that continent.

Greater variety

The variety of Australian marsupials has seemingly always been greater than that of South America—at least for the past several millions of years, for which the fossil record is good. Among the most interesting of the extinct species are *Thylacoleo,* the "marsupial lion," and *Thylacinus,* the "marsupial wolf." *Thylacinus* is of particular interest because it almost survived to the present day. It is thought to have been wiped out by European settlers, who not only destroyed its habitat, but hunted it aggressively. It finally succumbed to disease—the last known specimen died in a Tasmanian zoo in 1936.

A marked feature of the earlier marsupials of Australia was the

enormous size of many of the species. "Giant" kangaroos such as the short-faced *Procoptodon* were joined by a hippo-size wombat, *Diprotodon*. Living relatives of both of these are herbivores. But kangaroos in particular can be extremely aggressive when threatened. Their size and speed, in combination with such vigorous defensive behavior, might have made them difficult prey for the likes of *Thylacoleo* unless those predators hunted cooperatively.

Thylacoleo carnifex is commonly referred to as a marsupial lion. Although it had a much shorter body than the lion, it was a powerfully built animal. Estimates of its body weight range up to 360 lb (164 kg)—a large predator by any standards. The animal lacked developed canine teeth, but the upper incisors were enlarged to perform a similar role. In the cheeks, the third premolars became elongated shearing blades, enabling *Thylacoleo* to slice flesh efficiently.

FACT FILE

Genus: *Thylacoleo*

Species: *T. carnifex* illustrated

Shoulder height: 28 in (70 cm)

Head/body length: 45 in (115 cm)

Lived: Australia, 1.8 mya-30,000 ya

Left: *The highlighted areas of the map show the distribution of major populations of marsupials according to fossil finds of the Cenozoic era.*

Below: *A reconstruction of the partial skeleton of* Thylacoleo *from the Victoria Fossil Cave in Australia shows the powerful forelimbs and the likely method of grasping prey with the claws.*

49

Thylacoleo carnifex

HOLOCENE	present
	2,000 ya
	4,000 ya
	6,000 ya
	8,000 ya
	10,000 ya
PLEISTOCENE	0.2 mya
	0.4
	0.6
	0.8
	1 mya
	1.2
	1.4
	1.6
	1.8
	2 mya
PLIOCENE	3
	4
	5

Kangaroos

There are about 60 living species of kangaroos, mostly small. But some of the extinct ones were considerably bigger than today's largest.

Most living marsupials in Australia are fairly small. The red kangaroo may be the size of a man and is a powerful animal, but the majority of kangaroos found there are at the smaller end of the size range.

Gigantic creatures

Many of the fossil kangaroo species were comparatively gigantic creatures, especially members of the extinct subfamily Sthenurinae. These included the Pliocene and Pleistocene genera *Sthenurus, Procoptodon,* and *Simosthenurus.* The genus *Sthenurus* survived from 4 mya to 30,000 years ago. Like other marsupials,

Sthenurus stirlingi, reconstructed from deposits of 700,000 to 200,000 years ago, is the largest known member of its genus. It was powerfully built, with a short skull, long arms, and hands very well adapted for pulling down vegetation—a male standing on tiptoe could reach to about 10 ft (3 m). The term "giant" applied to such kangaroos is purely relative—the hind limbs are only slightly longer than those of a modern red kangaroo. But the bones are thicker and suggest a more massive body.

kangaroos are often seen as primitive compared with their placental counterparts. Indeed, in comparison with, say, an antelope, they do appear somewhat bizarre and even clumsy in their movements at slower speeds. But when moving fast they come into their own, able to travel at speeds of up to 37 mph (60 km/h). And in doing so they use less energy than a four-legged animal of similar size moving as fast. Whether the giant species were able to move particularly fast is an open question—they weighed more and might have sacrificed some speed for power.

Below: *This skeleton is of* Simosthenurus occidentalis, *a large extinct species of leaf-eating kangaroo. It is well represented by fossils in the Victoria Fossil Cave, South Australia. Note the short face and the single toe on the feet.*

FACT FILE

Genus: *Sthenurus*

Species: *S. stirlingi* illustrated

Height standing upright: 6 ft 6 in (2 m)

Lived: Australia, 0.7-0.2 mya

HOLOCENE	present
	2,000 ya
	4,000 ya
	6,000 ya
	8,000 ya
	10,000 ya
	0.2 mya
	0.4
	0.6
PLEISTOCENE	0.8
	1 mya
	1.2
	1.4
	1.6
	1.8
	2 mya
PLIOCENE	3
	4
	5

Marsupial lions (Thylacoleo) combine to hunt down the "giant" kangaroo
Sthenurus across the open plains of Australia some 30,000 years ago

Wombats

The giant Australian wombat Diprotodon optatum *was the size of a small car and is the largest of all known marsupials.*

Living wombats are fairly small animals, about the size of a beaver. They are burrowers, like marmots or badgers, and can be considered an enlarged version of a rodent. But just as the living kangaroos have giant fossil relatives, so too do the wombats. Many fossil wombats were the size of rhinos, and the largest was the size of a small car. This species, *Diprotodon optatum*, has often been characterized as a lumbering, rather slow-witted

animal. Such an idea is probably unavoidable, given its flat-footed stance and the rather blank facial appearance of many herbivores. But of course it had evolved to survive in its environment, just as other, more impressive-looking species have done.

Slow but relatively safe

The very diversity of the large wombats points to a measure of success in coping with the

Below: *The skull of the giant wombat clearly shows the grinding cheek teeth and forward placement of the incisors.*

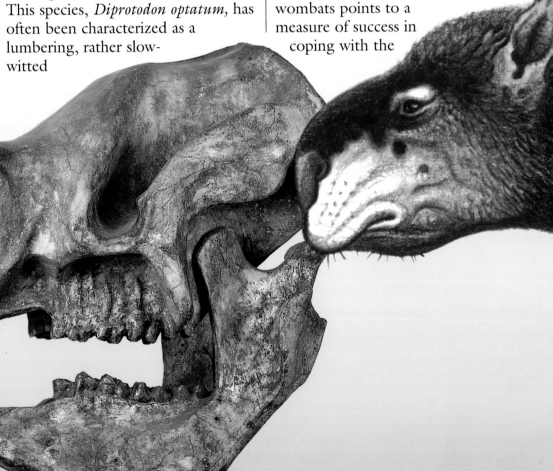

Australian habitats. Despite its evident lack of speed, the giant wombat is likely to have been fairly safe from predators. Its sheer size would have protected it in a continent where the largest known marsupial carnivore was *Thylacoleo carnifex*, the so-called marsupial lion. But the gigantic lizard *Megalania prisca* might have been a threat that size alone could not deter, particularly if it was able to administer a septic wound. And of course the young of even the largest species are always more at risk.

Diprotodon optatum is the largest of all known marsupials, possibly weighing 4 or 5 tons. This Pleistocene wombat was an ungainly creature, with very heavy limb bones and large feet, and must have moved fairly slowly. The jaws were powerful in a massively built skull. But that skull housed a small brain, and the jaws contained the broad, grinding cheek teeth of a herbivore. It probably plucked its food with its forward-set incisors, rather like a modern-day horse does.

FACT FILE

Genus: *Diprotodon*

Species: *D. optatum* illustrated

Shoulder height: 6 ft 6 in (2 m)

Head/body length: 10 ft (3 m)

Lived: Australia, 1.75 mya-10,000 ya

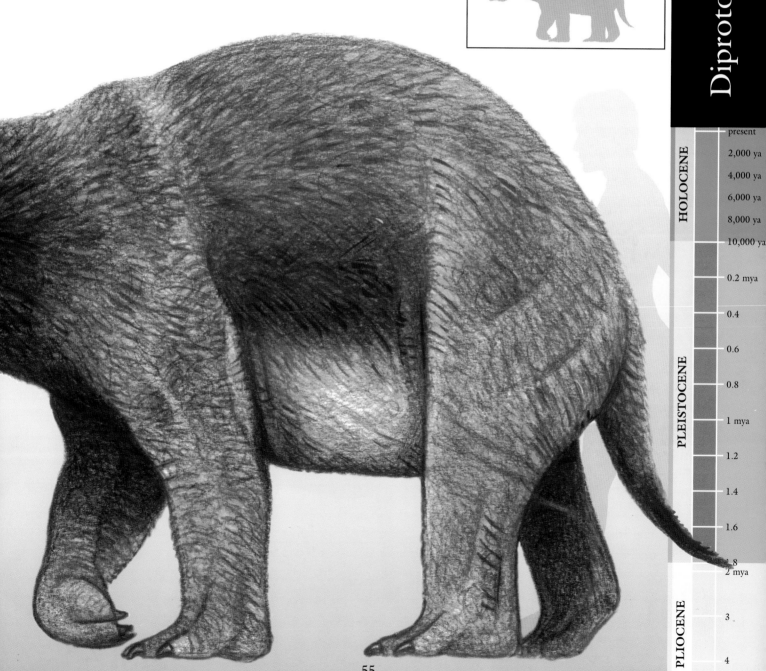

HOLOCENE	present
	2,000 ya
	4,000 ya
	6,000 ya
	8,000 ya
	10,000 ya
PLEISTOCENE	0.2 mya
	0.4
	0.6
	0.8
	1 mya
	1.2
	1.4
	1.6
	1.8
	2 mya
PLIOCENE	3
	4
	5

South American marsupials

South America once hosted a unique mixture of placental and marsupial mammals.

Thylacosmilus atrox is often referred to as the marsupial saber-toothed cat, a species of later Miocene and earlier Pliocene times. Unlike the teeth of placental saber-tooths, however, its two upper canines lay close together in the jaw, and were matched by large projections on the mandible, or lower jaw. These might have served to protect them from damage. The teeth were presumably used to slash and produce blood loss in the prey.

Like Australia, South America remained isolated during most of the Age of Mammals. However, unlike Australia, it later joined up to another landmass, North America. This joining was completed when, nearly 3 million years ago, a narrow corridor called the Panama Isthmus was formed. It provided a land bridge between the two continents. Marsupials evolved in South America before their counterparts in Australia. But whereas only marsupial mammals evolved in Australia, both placental and marsupial species developed alongside each other in considerable numbers in South America. Once the land reconnection occurred, a period of interchange of animals took place between North and South America. During this process, the unique mixture of South American species was gradually broken up. Many placental mammals and almost all of the marsupials were wiped out. Only a few, such as the successful omnivorous opossum *Didelphis*, managed to survive.

Predators

Before that happened, the South American marsupials had developed very differently from those of Australia. The Australian marsupials included both predators and herbivores, whereas the

FACT FILE

Genus: *Thylacosmilus*

Species: *T. atrox* illustrated

Shoulder height: 24 in (60 cm)

Head/body length: 55 in (140 cm)

Lived: Argentina, 7-2 mya

Thylacosmilus atrox

South American marsupials were mostly predators—carnivores and insectivores. The plant-eaters were found instead among the placental mammals. The best known of the marsupials among that rich diversity of animals are the saber-toothed *Thylacosmilus atrox* and the borhyaenids, a group of animals with a mixture of bearlike and doglike features. *Thylacosmilus* probably derived from the borhyaenids.

Thylacosmilus was outwardly similar to placental saber-toothed cats of other continents. The borhyaenids varied considerably in size, but they and *Thylacosmilus* all had relatively short legs. They placed their hind feet flat on the ground, like a bear does, in what is known as a plantigrade stance. In moving, this has the effect of shortening the hind limbs, reducing stride length and agility, and restricting speed. It suggests that, though powerful, none of these predators was particularly fast.

Borhyaena Borhyaenids resembled a cross between a dog and a bear, with the same range of sizes. The skull was long and heavy, with impressive canines and large, bone-smashing and meat-slicing cheek teeth. But like *Thylacosmilus*, *Borhyaena* had short limbs and adopted a plantigrade stance. As a result, they were unlikely to have been able to chase after prey.

FACT FILE

Genus: *Borhyaena*

Species: *B. tuberata* illustrated

Shoulder height: 14 in (36 cm)

Head/body length: 38 in (96 cm)

Lived: S. Argentina, 27-17 mya

Left: *The map shows the distribution of the two profiled mammals in South America.*

■ *Thylacosmilus atrox*

☐ *Borhyaena tuberata*

Above: *This skull of* Borhyaena tuberata *is 17 million years old. It was unearthed in southern Argentina. Note the length of the skull and its impressive canines.*

Borhyaena tuberata

Thylacosmilus atrox
Borhyaena tuberata

PLIOCENE — 1.8 / 2 mya / 3 / 4 / 5 mya

MIOCENE — 10 / 15 / 20 mya / 25

OLIGOCENE — 30 / 35

EOCENE — 40 mya / 45

Eomaia

Eomaia, discovered only recently in China's Liaoning Province, was about the size of a mouse. It is considered to be the earliest known placental mammal.

Eomaia scansoria The reconstructed appearance of *Eomaia* shows an animal somewhat similar to a living Asian tree shrew. It was a small animal, about the size of a mouse and weighing less than 1 ounce (25 g). Like all small mammals, it would have needed a plentiful supply of food to maintain its body temperature. Its climbing abilities would have given it every opportunity to find and catch insects, a highly nutritious source of food, among the vegetation.

Right: *The remains of* Eomaia *show the clear detail of teeth, feet, and hair captured in the fine sediments.*

The tiny *Eomaia scansoria* is preserved in such exquisite detail that its teeth, feet, and even its hair can be seen in the fossil. The degree of preservation is not surprising, as it was found in the same ancient lake bed in China as the now famous feathered dinosaurs. Feathers, like hair, are preserved only in exceptionally fine-grained deposits. The deposits date back to the earlier part of the Cretaceous period, 125 million years ago.

Climbing ability

Eomaia is thought to be a placental mammal, and is thus the earliest known representative of the group. Its long digits and strongly curved claws have led researchers to suggest it was a proficient climber. It appears to have lived on the shores of a lake, where it probably fed on insects.

FACT FILE

Genus: *Eomaia*

Species: *E. scansoria* illustrated

Shoulder height: Less than 1 in (2 cm)

Head/body length: Less than 5 in (12 cm)

Lived: China, 125 mya

Eomaia scansoria

Aardvarks

The name aardvark is Afrikaans and means earth pig, a fair description of an animal that spends its life digging in the ground.

The living aardvark, *Orycteropus afer*, is widely distributed in Africa south of the Sahara. It is well equipped for digging to obtain its main food of termites. Its teeth, which lack enamel, grow continuously, so are not destroyed by the grit that must accompany each mouthful of food.

Aardvarks are known from Miocene localities (24-5 mya) in the eastern part of Africa, and the aardvark is thought most probably to have originated in that continent. But Miocene remains have also been found in Eurasia, particularly in Greece, where the smaller and less robust *Orycteropus gaudryi* occurs.

Material from early Miocene deposits has been referred to the genus *Myorycteropus*. A further genus, *Leptorycteropus*, has recently been found in later Miocene deposits.

Leptorycteropus guilielmi
This late Miocene aardvark from Lothagam in eastern Africa is known only from fragmentary material. Like *Myorycteropus*, it was smaller than the living species, perhaps half its size. It had the typically curved back of an aardvark but was lighter in build, with less muscular limbs and a shorter nose. All of these features suggest it was less specialized as a digger. It might have sought food items more readily found on the surface.

Right: Orycteropus depereti, *from early Pliocene deposits near Perpignan in France, is the latest known European aardvark.*

FACT FILE

Genus: *Leptorycteropus*

Species: *L. guilielmi*

Head/body length: 18 in (45 cm)

Lived: Eastern Africa, 8-6 mya

Eomaia Leptorycteropus guilielmi

Leptorycteropus guilielmi

59

5 mya
10
MIOCENE
15
20 mya
25
OLIGO.
30
35
40 mya
EOCENE
45
50
55
PALEO.
60
65
85
CRETACEOUS
105
125

Sea cows and relatives

Here are two groups of marine mammals related to elephants—sea cows and desmostylians.

Halitherium schinzi is a sirenian fossil species commonly found in the Oligocene of Europe, with complete skeletons in Germany and elsewhere. Although it probably had no external rear limb, the fossils show evidence of a basic femur (thighbone) that joined a reduced pelvis. The front flippers were evidently small. This would suggest a broad, flattened tail if the animal was to be able to move through the water with any speed.

The extinct desmostylians and the fossil and living sirenians—the sea cows—are distinct orders of animals that are thought to be related to each other. It is fairly well established that both groups are closely related to the elephants. The desmostylids, which are known from Oligocene and Miocene deposits of the northern Pacific Ocean, are perhaps more easy to envisage as elephant relatives

because they had limbs. These were large and paddlelike, however, and suggest an aquatic lifestyle. Better analogies might be with something like a hippopotamus.

Unusual teeth

The teeth are unlike those of any living group. One of the best specimens of a desmostylid is that of *Paleoparadoxia*

Right: *A skeleton of* Halitherium schinzi *from the Stuttgart Museum shows the poorly developed rear limb and short front flippers that typify this desmostylid. Note also the heavy and elongated rib cage. The added weight and increased lung capacity together would have provided fine control of buoyancy in animals that were probably not active divers.*

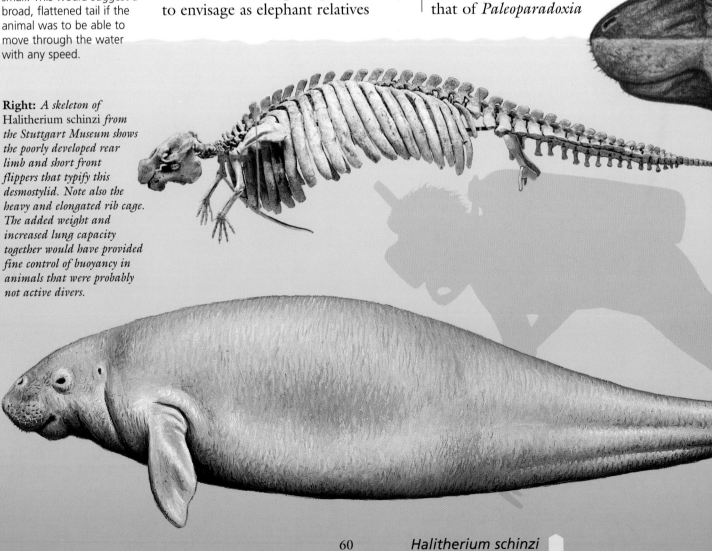

Halitherium schinzi

tabatai, found in 1964 during excavations at the campus of Stanford University in California.

Sea cows

Sea cows, of which the dugongs and manatees are still living, are less easy to envisage as elephant relatives. They are large animals that lack rear limbs, and look if anything like a cross between a whale and a seal. They are known from earliest Eocene deposits of Hungary. Finds of the genus *Halitherium* are common in Oligocene deposits in Europe. The genus *Metaxytherium* contains several species found variously in Miocene deposits as far apart as Florida and the Mediterranean Sea.

Paleoparadoxia tabatai is a common Miocene fossil desmostylian in marine deposits. The well-developed limbs suggest an ability to move on land and in water. But the large feet might have made movement out of water rather awkward, perhaps like a sea lion. The cheek teeth, with many pillars, and large, forward-facing canines could mean that it rooted for and fed on water-edge plants rather than seaweed.

FACT FILE

Genus: *Halitherium*
Species: *H. schinzi* illustrated
Length: 8 ft 8 in (2.65 m)
Lived: Europe, 35-24 mya

Genus: *Paleoparadoxia*
Species: *P. tabatai* illustrated
Shoulder height: 5 ft 2 in (1.57 m)
Lived: North Pacific, 30-12 mya

61   *Paleoparadoxia tabatai*

MIOCENE	5 mya
	10
	15
	20 mya
OLIGOCENE	25
	30
	35
EOCENE	40 mya
	45
	50
	55
PALEOCENE	60 mya
	65

Deinotheres

The proboscids, or trunked mammals, were once more diverse than they are today. In addition to the elephantids, the only living family, they included the deinotheres, mastodons, and mammoths.

The order Proboscidea, or proboscids, probably originated in Africa, and began to disperse to Eurasia in the early Miocene epoch, some 24 million years ago. They are represented today only by the Indian and African elephants, and by a possible third species, the forest elephant from central Africa. These are all members of the elephantids, the only living family. The early fossil history of proboscids contains a more diverse array of families, including the deinotheres,

Below: *A mounted skeleton of the early Miocene* Deinotherium bavaricum, *in the Stuttgart Museum, clearly shows the elongated neck and head of these animals, set upon an otherwise elephant-like body.*

mastodons, and mammoths—all possessing trunks and tusks.

No upper tusks

Although elephant-like in size and structure, the deinotheres differed from the other proboscids in that they had no upper tusks. In addition, the tusks in the lower jaw have a distinctive downward curve. The deinotheres might have used these for pulling up plants.

Deinotheres are very common in the African fossil record, especially in the Pliocene of eastern areas, with the species *Deinotherium bozasi*. In Eurasia, the best known species are *D. bavaricum* and *D. giganteum,* the largest member of the family.

Deinotherium giganteum, from the middle Miocene of Eurasia, is the largest known member of the family, with a shoulder height approaching 12 ft (3.5 m). The nasal area of the skull clearly indicates the presence of a trunk, although whether it was as long and as efficiently controlled as that of a living elephant is uncertain. The low-crowned teeth with rounded cusps suggest a browsing diet, and the tusks on the lower jaw perhaps served to pull at vegetation.

Right: *The jaw of* Deinotherium *emphasizes the size and arrangement of the tusks.*

FACT FILE

Genus: *Deinotherium*

Species: *D. giganteum* illustrated

Shoulder height: Over 11 ft 6 in (3.5 m)

Lived: Eurasia, 17-1.6 mya

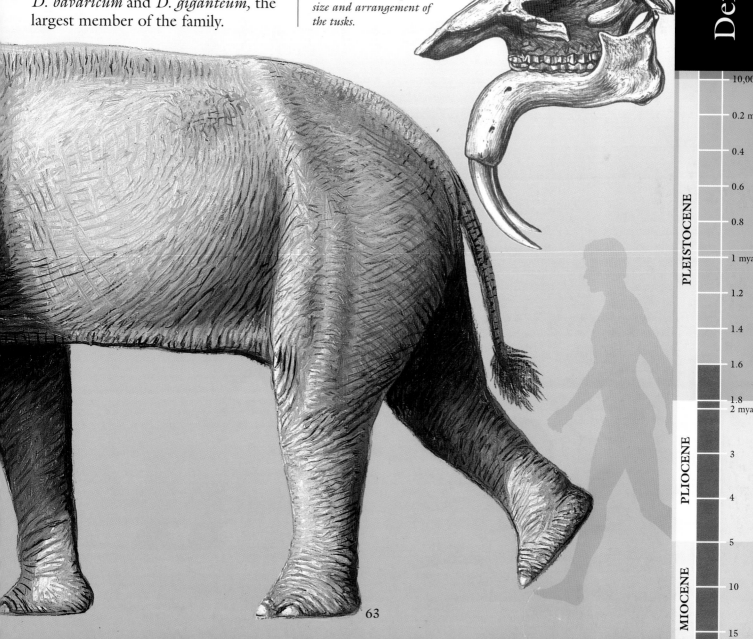

Deinotherium

	10,000 ya
PLEISTOCENE	0.2 mya
	0.4
	0.6
	0.8
	1 mya
	1.2
	1.4
	1.6
	1.8
	2 mya
PLIOCENE	3
	4
	5
MIOCENE	10
	15

Gomphotheres

Trunked mammals, the gomphotheres and mammutids, first appeared in Europe about 20 million years ago. Gomphotherium *was a "four-tusker," but the later* Anancus *had only two.*

Gomphotherium angustidens Individuals of this species were about the size of a living Indian elephant. But their bodies were more elongated, with relatively short limbs. The upper tusks were moderately developed. The animal also had a very extended lower jaw bearing a pair of shorter tusks. These might have been used for digging at soft vegetation, perhaps in water.

Below: *A herd of* Anancus arvernensis *drinking at an early Pliocene water hole. This animal had only the upper tusks, and looked much more like a living elephant.*

The mastodons, literally meaning "nipple-toothed" and named for the raised form of the biting surfaces of the teeth, comprise two families of proboscids. These are the gomphotheres and the mammutids, both of which appear to have originated in Africa. The gomphotheres are widely known, and early forms might have given rise to the true elephants. Early gomphotheres are particularly well represented by the genus *Gomphotherium*. Species of *Gomphotherium* had an elongated skull, lower tusks at the end of a very long mandible (jaw), and only moderately developed upper tusks.

In contrast, later gomphotheres, such as members of the genus *Anancus*, show a good example of the common evolutionary phenomenon of convergence. The general shortening of the skull, reduction and loss of lower tusks, and development of long and straight upper tusks all make them look more superficially like the true elephants. Although they retained the relatively short legs of *Gomphotherium*, even those had to lengthen in order to compensate for the increased length of the upper tusks.

Left: Gomphotherium angustidens *spread through the Mediterranean countries of Europe and as far north as Germany.*

Right: *A small herd of* Gomphotherium angustidens *cool themselves in the early Miocene lake at Els Cassots, in Spain.*

FACT FILE

Genus: *Gomphotherium*

Species: *G. angustidens* illustrated

Shoulder height: 6 ft 6 in (2 m)

Lived: Southern and central Europe, 18-12 mya

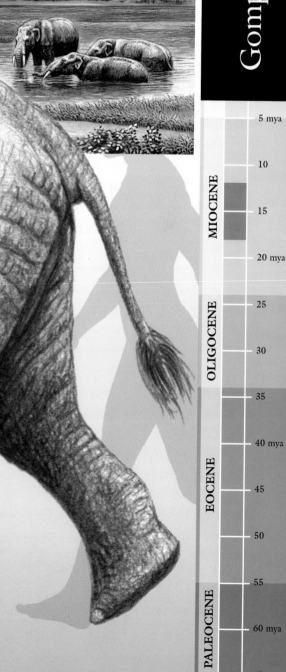

MIOCENE	5 mya
	10
	15
	20 mya
OLIGOCENE	25
	30
	35
EOCENE	40 mya
	45
	50
PALEOCENE	55
	60 mya
	65

True mastodons

The "true" mastodons belong to the Mammutidae family but shouldn't be confused with mammoths. Mammut americanum colonized North America, where it coexisted with the woolly mammoth.

The second family of mastodons, what may be termed the true mastodons, are more advanced forms belonging to the proboscidian family Mammutidae. Because of that name they are sometimes confused with the similar-sounding mammoths. But they were very different animals.

Colonizing the New World

Like the gomphotheres, the true mastodons had cheek teeth with low and rounded crowns. This indicated a browsing diet, although with some adaptations to coping with more abrasive foods. And like the later gomphothere *Anancus,* they had shorter faces and had lost the lower tusks, making them more superficially like the true elephants.

Mastodons also managed to colonize the New World, where *Mammut americanum* coexisted alongside mammoths and is known on the basis of several largely complete specimens. Both appear to have been hunted in some quantities by human groups entering North America about 12,000 years ago.

European forms

The largest members of the genus are the European forms, especially *Mammut borsoni.* This animal reached

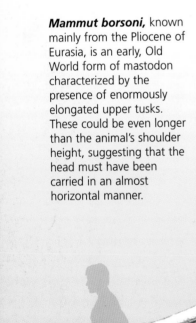

Mammut borsoni, known mainly from the Pliocene of Eurasia, is an early, Old World form of mastodon characterized by the presence of enormously elongated upper tusks. These could be even longer than the animal's shoulder height, suggesting that the head must have been carried in an almost horizontal manner.

Mammut borsoni

Left: *A distribution map of regions inhabited by* Mammut borsoni *(Europe) and* M. americanum *(Central and North America).*

☐ *Mammut borsoni* ■ *Mammut americanum*

11 feet 6 inches (3.5 m) at the shoulder based on material from Milia in Greece. *M. borsoni* was very common in the early Pliocene fauna (range of animals) of Europe. However, with the appearance there of elephants about 2.5 million years ago, it gradually died out.

Mammut americanum is a Central and North American species from the Pleistocene. These mastodons were generally smaller than their Old World relatives, with a shoulder height of 8 ft (2.5 m) or more, and the tusks were of more moderate size. The latest examples coexisted with the earliest human inhabitants of the continent and were hunted by them. Some remarkable fossils found in bog deposits even include vestiges of body hair and remains of their last meals.

FACT FILE

Genus: *Mammut*

Species: *M. borsoni* illustrated

Shoulder height: 11 ft 6 in (3.5 m)

Lived: Europe, 5.5-2.5 mya

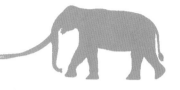

Genus: *Mammut*

Species: *M. americanum* illustrated

Shoulder height: 8 ft (2.5 m)

Lived: North and Central America, 1.6 mya-10,000 ya

Left: *A mounted skeleton of* Mammut americanum *in the Natural History Museum in London.*

Mammut borsoni
Mammut americanum

PLEISTOCENE

PLIOCENE

MIOCENE

10,000 ya
0.2 mya
0.4
0.6
0.8
1 mya
1.2
1.4
1.6
1.8
2 mya
3
4
5
10
15

Mammut americanum

Elephantids

Elephants are the largest living land mammals, but the extinct African species Elephas recki *was even larger. One specimen stood 3 feet higher at the shoulder than the tallest living elephant.*

Above: *A partial skeleton of* Elephas recki. *Among the items exposed are a tusk, two shoulder blades, limb bones, and ribs.*

The true elephants are members of the family Elephantidae, or elephantids. This includes the living African and Asian species and the mammoths. Some of the most important elephant fossils come from Africa, where they have a good fossil record. The best specimens are of Pliocene age (5-1.8 mya), but the record dates back to later Miocene times at about 8 million years ago.

Elephants differ from gomphotheres and mammutids in being longer-legged, with a very short and high skull. The teeth are also much higher crowned, with numerous ridges of hard enamel running from side to side across the biting surface. These patterns indicate increasing adaptation to cope with tough vegetation. This is particularly evident in successive populations of the now extinct African species *Elephas recki* during the later Pliocene (2 mya). The living Asian (or Indian) genus *Elephas* originated in Africa, and its fossils are common in the eastern part of the continent.

Right: *A scene to the east of Lake Turkana in northern Kenya, during the early Pleistocene, about 1.5 mya. This view shows a river channel near the point where it joined the lake during the dry season. A herd of* Elephas recki *move toward the lake accompanied by antelopes.*

Left: *Fossil remains of Elephas recki have been found throughout most of eastern Africa.*

Elephas recki had the short, high head of the modern Asian elephant (*E. maximus*), but with a more domed forehead. A nearly complete skeleton from Koobi Fora, near Lake Turkana in Kenya, shows an animal with a small head and tusks, long forelimbs, and low eye sockets—unlike any living species.

FACT FILE

Genus: *Elephas*
Species: *E. recki* illustrated
Length: 15 ft (4.5 m)
Lived: Africa, 4-0.5 mya

HOLOCENE

present
2,000 ya
4,000 ya
6,000 ya
8,000 ya
10,000 ya

0.2 mya

0.4

0.6

0.8

1 mya

1.2

1.4

1.6

1.8
2 mya

PLEISTOC

3

4

5

PLIOCENE

Mammoths

The woolly mammoth is perhaps one of the most familiar fossil mammals. Its bones have been found in enormous quantities, and its appearance has been depicted in European cave art.

Mammuthus primigenius, the woolly mammoth, is one of the best known of all fossil mammals. Adaptations to the cold of ice age climates such as a compact build were matched by a warm coat of hair and small ears that would reduce heat loss and danger from frostbite. Even the anus was protected by a disklike flap on the tail that shut out the cold.

Below: *A herd of mammoths watch as a group of lions pass by, more interested in the reindeer to the left of the picture.*

Mammoths, like other elephants, originated in Africa. They emigrated from there about 3 million years ago. They spread across Europe and Asia and into North America, where they dispersed as far south as Central America. Mammoth bones and teeth are extremely common fossils. But we know the latest of the line, *Mammuthus primigenius,* not only from its fossils, but also from cave art and preserved remains of carcasses. Such carcasses are found from time to time in the frozen deposits of Alaska and Siberia. (See

the picture of the baby mammoth on page 33.)

Mammoth teeth are among the most highly evolved of all elephantid teeth. They have a complex series of ridges of dental enamel, the hardest material in the body, containing elongated islands of bonelike dentine. The enamel wears more slowly than the dentine, producing a constant series of raised areas rather like a

70

file. As a result, when the upper and lower teeth came together, they were able to grind even the most abrasive plant materials. The mammoth fossil record in Europe and the Americas shows the progressive evolution of this feature, which culminated in the teeth of the woolly mammoth. The largest teeth had as many as 30 parallel ridges.

Soft tissues

Frozen remains provide an insight also into the soft tissues of the animal. It had thick body fat and a long, dense coat of hair with a softer underpelt. The long tusks were probably used to clear snow from vegetation, and perhaps to dig for roots and tubers.

Below: *A mounted skeleton in the Stuttgart Museum shows the strong and compact build of the woolly mammoth and the straight, pillarlike legs typical of heavy mammals. The wide spread of the ribs indicates the massive size of the chest and abdominal cavities. A huge stomach was essential for the bulky digestive system needed to cope with the large amounts of food taken in.*

FACT FILE

Genus: *Mammuthus*

Species: *M. primigenius*

Shoulder height: 10 ft (3 m)

Lived: Eurasia and North America, 120,000–10,000 ya

HOLOCENE

present
2,000 ya
4,000 ya
6,000 ya
8,000 ya
10,000 ya
0.2 mya
0.4
0.6
0.8
1 mya
1.2
1.4
1.6
1.8
2 mya

PLEISTOCENE

PLIOCENE

3

4

5

71

Elephantids

A group of woolly mammoths trundle across a late Pleistocene landscape in what is now northern Spain. Also in this Ice Age scene are equids (left), a woolly rhinoceros (right), and cave lions with a reindeer carcass.

Arsinoitheres

The only species in its family, Arsinoitherium zitteli *bears similarities to both elephants and rhinoceroses, but it is unrelated to either.*

Arsinoitherium zitteli
resembled a rhinoceros in size and appearance, although the skeleton and, in particular, the limbs were rather elephant-like in their proportions. The head was much more rhinolike, although it differed in having a paired set of large, bony horn cores attached to the skull. Each of these had a single smaller knob set at its rear border. And they were probably covered in a sheath of horn made of keratinized skin, as is seen in the horns of cattle.

The arsinoitheres are the only family in the extinct order of Embrithopoda. This is one of the most unusual groups of animals, with no known descendants and no clear ancestors. It is only really known from the Oligocene deposits of the Fayum Depression in Egypt, and is based on a single species, *Arsinoitherium zitteli*. Arsinoitheres were plant-eating animals that lived in the well-wooded conditions of the Fayum in what appears to have been a coastal floodplain with mangrove swamps, slow-moving streams, and

ponds. Specimens from Turkey, Romania, and even Mongolia have been linked with the Egyptian species, but they seem to come from much smaller and more primitive animals. And none is represented by anything more than jaw fragments.

The teeth of arsinoitheres include relatively small incisors and lack tusks or elongated canines.

The cheek teeth were fairly high-crowned, and look more like those of a browsing animal than a grazer. The elongated limbs suggest an animal able to move easily over distances and perhaps with some speed. The large, five-toed feet would give good support in wetter conditions and perhaps suggest a liking for aquatic environments.

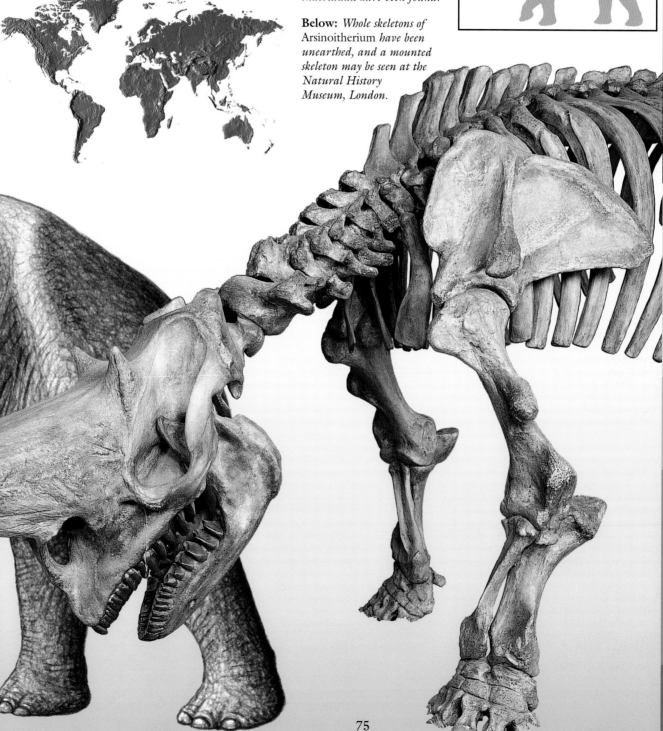

Left: *Remains of* Arsinoitherium *come from the Fayum Depression, to the west of the Nile River in northern Egypt. Many individuals have been found.*

Below: *Whole skeletons of* Arsinoitherium *have been unearthed, and a mounted skeleton may be seen at the Natural History Museum, London.*

FACT FILE

Genus: *Arsinoitherium*

Species: *A. zitteli*

Shoulder height: 6 ft (1.8 m)

Lived: Egypt, 36-30 mya

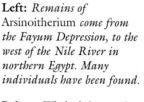

5 mya

10

MIOCENE

15

20 mya

25

OLIGOCENE

30

35

40 mya

EOCENE

45

50

55

PALEOCENE

60 mya

65

Two Arsinoitherium cross a river in the tropical Oligocene forest of what is now northern Egypt, some 50 miles (80 km) southwest of Cairo. These unique creatures were herbivores, living on leafy vegetation.

Sloths

Gigantic ground sloths were among the largest land mammals of South and North America. Some of them, such as Megatherium americanum, *reached huge proportions.*

Megatherium americanum, the American giant ground sloth known from Argentina to Texas, was a truly enormous animal, up to 20 feet (6 m) in length. The massive skeleton and equally massive and exceptionally broad pelvis suggest a slow-moving animal capable of standing on or even squatting on its hind legs while using its front feet to pull at vegetation. As in *Nothrotheriops,* complete skeletons and naturally mummified remains are known with skin, tendons, and pelt attached to the bones.

Edentate means "without teeth," and is the name given to a peculiar order of South American mammals, the Edentata, that includes the armadillos, sloths, and anteaters. Not all lack teeth. But some have reduced numbers and may lack the hard enamel coating on those that remain. Living sloths and armadillos are fairly strange creatures to most observers. But the fossil edentates include truly bizarre forms, such as the ground sloths and the glyptodonts (see pages 80-81).

Ground sloths were very diverse, but the best known are the larger species. Some of these managed to colonize North America, where perhaps the best examples are *Nothrotheriops shastensis* and the truly gigantic *Megatherium americanum.* The last of them died out around the end of the last glaciation, or ice age, about 10,000 years ago. Dung and even portions of pelt are known to have been preserved in caves in drier areas. The feet were equipped with large claws. These physical features, together with the vast array of plant remains recovered from the dung

Megatherium americanum

Left: *Known distributions of* Megatherium *and* Nothrotheriops *in the Americas.*

☐ *Megatherium*   ■ *Nothrotheriops*

Nothrotheriops shastensis, a medium-size ground sloth species of North and Central America, is found, among other sites, at the famous La Brea Tar Pits in Los Angeles. It was a much smaller animal than *Megatherium,* measuring 7-8 ft (2.1-2.4 m) long. But the body build was essentially the same as its larger relatives'.

Below: *The massive size of* Megatherium *can be gauged by the deer passing in front of the tree.*

deposits, point to a diet of arid-region or desert plants, as well as temperate-region trees such as pine, birch, and juniper. All of these presumably were consumed according to season. Most reconstructions accordingly show the ground sloths squatting on their haunches and pulling down higher branches from trees.

FACT FILE

Genus: *Megatherium*

Species: *M. americanum*

Shoulder height: 7 ft (2.1 m)

Lived: South America, 4 mya-10,000 ya; North America, 1.8 mya-10,000 ya

Genus: *Nothrotheriops*

Species: *N. shastensis*

Shoulder height: 4 ft (1.2 m)

Lived: North and Central America, 2 mya-10,000 ya

Nothrotheriops shastensis ■   79

HOLOCENE	present
	2,000 ya
	4,000 ya
	6,000 ya
	8,000 ya
	10,000 ya
	0.2 mya
	0.4
	0.6
PLEISTOCENE	0.8
	1 mya
	1.2
	1.4
	1.6
	1.8
	2 mya
PLIOCENE	3
	4
	5

Glyptodonts

Despite looking like something from the age of dinosaurs, glyptodonts are in fact fossil mammals, with an outer case of "armor plating." The largest weighed more than a ton.

Glyptotherium, one of the largest of the glyptodonts, was a tanklike, quite slow-moving animal. It would usually have been immune to attack by even the largest of the placental and marsupial predators that lived alongside it. However, one find of a skull in Florida, with holes corresponding in size to the canine teeth of a jaguar, shows that in some circumstances even these heavily armored creatures fell prey to the big cats.

Among the strangest of all mammals in the fossil record are the members of the South American family Glyptodontidae, or glyptodonts. They are related to the living armadillos, whose carapace—a shell-like bony covering—consists of numerous flexible bands. But the glyptodonts had a single, inflexible, and often massive body carapace made up of hexagonal (six-sided) bony plates and a smaller shield on the skull. These plates actually grew within the skin rather than in addition to and on top of it. Because of their bulky construction, they fossilized extremely well. Specimens have been found ranging in length from less than 20 inches (50 cm) to over 10 feet (3 m) in the case of *Doedicurus*.

The glyptodont skeleton—and in particular the vertebrae of the spinal column—was highly modified to provide a rigid, load-bearing structure. The limbs were short and the feet large. The cheek teeth were high-crowned but lacked enamel—a deficiency made up for by their continuous growth. There

Left: *Although glyptodonts were confined mainly to South America, the genus* Glyptotherium *did manage to disperse into the southern part of North America.*

Below right: *A skeleton and carapace of* Glyptotherium *in the Natural History Museum in London.*

Below: *The South American glyptodont* Doedicurus *was built like a tank and weighed more than a ton. It would probably have used its club-tail in self-defense.*

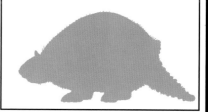

were no incisors. So glyptodonts probably lived on a diet of relatively soft but perhaps gritty food.

Glyptodonts have a long fossil history in South America and achieved quite a diversity of species there. But they reached their greatest size during the Pliocene and Pleistocene epochs. Some of the largest were members of the genus *Glyptotherium*, in which the huge plate of armorlike bone could be more than 6 feet (2 m) long. *Glyptotherium* managed to migrate as far north as Oklahoma, in North America, as part of the interchange of animals between the two continents.

present
2,000 ya
4,000 ya
6,000 ya
8,000 ya
10,000 ya

HOLOCENE

0.2 mya

0.4

0.6

0.8

1 mya

1.2

1.4

1.6

1.8
2 mya

PLEISTOCENE

3

4

PLIOCENE

5

Rodents

About a third of the living species of mammals are rodents. Among the rich variety of fossil forms are large species that hopped like small kangaroos.

The order Rodentia—the rodents—is one of the most successful in the history of mammal evolution. There are more than 1,600 identified species, or about one-third of living mammal species. They range in size from capybaras— 4 feet (1.2 m) long—down through squirrels to tiny mice. Most are small animals that lead highly active lives.

Gnawing teeth

Rodents eat a variety of food items, and their defining feature is their specialized teeth. These are the continuously growing incisors that enable them to gnaw their way through a range of tough materials. Beavers, as is well known, can even bring down trees.

As with other smaller mammals, the fossil record of rodents is extremely patchy. However, many rodent groups are found in their own particular habitat, so their presence in a deposit may offer numerous clues to past environmental conditions. Pellets regurgitated by birds of prey such as owls can provide further clues about fossil rodents and their habitats.

Most rodents move on four legs, but some, such as the gerbils, hop. Fossil species such as *Pseudoltinomys gaillardi* show this to be an ancient adaptation. The springhare family, or the Pedetidae, are the largest living rodents with a hopping style of locomotion. Extinct members of the family, such as

Megapedetes pentadactylus, from the lower Miocene of Songhor in Kenya, is the largest known member of the springhare family. Although primitive in some ways compared with living relatives, it had similar body proportions and features. These indicate a hopping gait as in the modern springhare, *Pedetes capensis.* This form of locomotion, familiar in kangaroos, combines speed with a great economy of energy.

Megapedetes pentadactylus

Megapedetes, were even larger, although otherwise very similar to their modern counterparts.

Recent finds in South America have extended the size range of prehistoric rodents to that of a buffalo. A specimen from Venezuela named *Phoberomys pattersoni* is thought to have been twice as long and weighed eight times as much as the capybara.

Pseudoltinomys gaillardi belongs to an extinct family of Old World rodents. A beautifully preserved skeleton from southern France even shows traces of tail hairs. The creature was about the size of a rat. Its long hind legs suggest that it was an accomplished jumper that hopped, perhaps rather like a gerbil. It appears to have lived in relatively open habitats.

Below left: *A drawing of the* Pseudoltinomys gaillardi *skeleton found in Céreste, in the south of France.*

FACT FILE

Genus: *Megapedetes*

Species: *M. pentadactylus* illustrated

Head/body length: 20 in (50 cm)

Lived: Africa, 17 mya

Genus: *Pseudoltinomys*

Species: *P. gaillardi* illustrated

Head/body length: 8.3 in (21 cm)

Lived: Europe, 30 mya

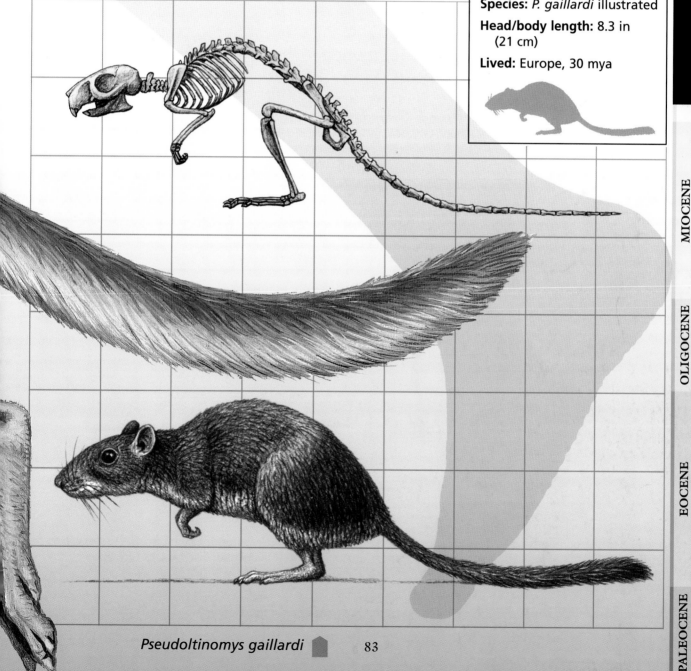

Pseudoltinomys gaillardi

83

MIOCENE	5 mya
	10
	15
	20 mya
OLIGOCENE	25
	30
	35
EOCENE	40 mya
	45
	50
	55
PALEOCENE	60 mya
	65

Early primates

The primates, clever and adaptable animals that include monkeys, apes, and humans, originated more than 65 mya. The first primates were small animals and their fossil record is poor.

Below: *A skull of the European late Eocene adapid primate* Adapis parisiensis, *from southern France.*

Plesiadapis tricuspidens, a primitive, rather squirrel-like animal, is known from late Paleocene deposits in Europe. Its robust skeleton has limb proportions like those of a terrestrial animal. It has claws instead of nails and rather rodentlike teeth. For these reasons, its status as a true early primate has been questioned.

The primates, the order to which monkeys, apes, and humans belong, is a diverse one containing more than 200 living species distributed in mostly tropical areas. Primates have relatively large brains, stereoscopic and color vision, and grasping hands and feet with a good sense of touch. Most have nails rather than claws, and a mobile shoulder joint. The combination of these features allows primates to live in a range of habitats. It enables some to live in trees, where they are able to move quickly and securely from branch to branch, are relatively safe from predators, and have good access to food.

Most living species are found in Africa, where 25 genera and some 70 species are known, with smaller numbers in Asia and South America. The order probably originated in the Northern Hemisphere more than 65 mya, in North America or Asia. The so-called protoprimate genus *Purgatorius* is known from earliest Paleocene deposits of North America, but whether this is a true primate is controversial.

The earliest stages of

FACT FILE

Genus: *Plesiadapis*

Species: *P. tricuspidens* illustrated

Shoulder height: 10 in (25 cm)

Lived: Europe, 60-55 mya

Plesiadapis tricuspidens

84

primate evolution have proved difficult to reconstruct. This is partly because they were fairly small animals and lived in woodlands—neither of which tends to ensure high representation in the fossil record. Among candidates as the ancestors to the earliest true primates in Europe are the plesiadapiformes. These are known from Paleocene deposits, most notably in the form of *Plesiadapis tricuspidens*. But in many ways they are rather more rodentlike in several features. Another possible ancestor, from the mid-Eocene of North America, is *Notharctus tenebrosus*, a member of the family Adapidae.

Notharctus tenebrosus, a North American member of the family Adapidae, is known from early-middle Eocene deposits. Specimens include a fairly complete skeleton. It shows the probable primitive form for the whole family, with long hind limbs and tail. It was probably well adapted for climbing and leaping from branch to branch in a lemurlike manner.

Below: *A scene depicting adapid primates of the* Agerinia *genus drinking from a forest water hole in early Eocene southern Europe.*

FACT FILE

Genus: *Notharctus*

Species: *N. tenebrosus* illustrated

Shoulder height: 8 in (20 cm)

Lived: North America, 51-46 mya

Notharctus tenebrosus

85

5 mya

10

15

MIOCENE

20 mya

25

OLIGOCENE

30

35

40 mya

EOCENE

45

50

55

PALEOCENE

60 mya

65

Monkeys

The monkeys are the largest group in the primates. They are found mostly in Africa, but also live in South and Central America and Asia. The largest fossil monkeys are of the genus Theropithecus.

Above: *A cast of the skull of a male* Theropithecus brumpti. *This shows its large canine teeth and prominent cheekbones.*

Below: *A pair of* Dolicopithecus *monkeys observe life around them from a branch.*

Monkeys are conventionally divided into Old and New World groups. New World monkeys, family Ceboidea, now live chiefly in South and Central America. They are distinguished by widely spaced nostrils, and many have prehensile tails. Such tails are able to act almost like an extra hand or foot, curling around branches or even picking up small objects. Old World monkeys, family Cercopithecidae, have closer-set nostrils and also have tails, but these lack prehensile capabilities.

The Cercopithecidae—the largest primate family—with more than 70 living species, include the acrobatic central and eastern African colobines. These animals eat leaves. They either lack thumbs or have almost lost them. They use their hands as a hook while moving through the trees. This indicates a long history of life in the forests. Others, members of the subfamily Cercopithecinae, or cheek-pouched monkeys, include smaller species such as the vervets as well as the more ground-living baboons, members of the genera *Papio* and *Theropithecus*.

The genus *Theropithecus*

The baboons are the largest living monkeys. Today only one species of baboon, the gelada from the Ethiopian highlands, belongs to the genus *Theropithecus*. But in the past this was a much more diverse group, with at least three very large species, including *T. brumpti*. The males of this species had huge canines, suggesting male display and threat behavior. And the cheekbones flared outward, suggesting the attachment of powerful chewing muscles. A marked feature of the hand in living and fossil theropithecines is the arrangement of the thumb and relatively short index

finger. These operate independently of the rest of the fingers to permit a strong and precise pincer movement. This enables them to select small food items such as the leaves of grasses and sometimes insects.

Theropithecus brumpti has a skeleton that shows many features of a ground-living animal, such as the powerful fore and aft movements of the limbs, mixed with some features of a tree-dweller, such as the flexibility and mobility of the shoulder joint. This combination serves to emphasize that tree-dwelling is not the only lifestyle for a primate.

Left: *Known distributions of the monkey* Theropithecus brumpti *in eastern Africa.*

FACT FILE

Genus: *Theropithecus*
Species: *T. brumpti* illustrated
Shoulder height: 35 in (90 cm)
Lived: Eastern Africa, 3.5-1.8 mya

Theropithecus brumpti

present
2,000 ya
4,000 ya
6,000 ya
8,000 ya
10,000 ya

0.2 mya

0.4

0.6

0.8

1 mya

1.2

1.4

1.6

1.8
2 mya

PLEIS

3

PLIOCENE

4

5

Apes

Early apes appear in the fossil record of Africa some 25 million years ago. They are thought to have adapted to living in tropical woodland.

Above: *A skull of* Proconsul africanus *held in the Natural History Museum in London.*

Proconsul africanus is known on the basis of relatively complete remains from Rusinga Island, on the eastern shore of Lake Victoria. It moved among the trees on four legs, more like a type of monkey than a living African ape.

Modern humans evolved from the apes, just as modern apes did. So living apes may be considered as our cousins, rather than our ancestors as is often mistakenly said.

Humans last shared a common ancestor with the African apes perhaps 6 to 7 million years ago. The earliest known African apes are placed in the separate family Proconsulidae, which takes its name from the genus *Proconsul* (illustrated here). These varied from the size of large monkeys up to small apes. They showed the general features of probable monkeylike ancestors, and moved on all fours. This suggests that they lived in the trees.

The stage after the proconsulids marks a further branching off, between 17 and 12 mya, of a group placed in the subfamily Dryopithecinae, or dryopithecines. These animals were sufficiently advanced to be classified as hominids, members of the family Hominidae. The family also includes humans and close fossil relatives, as well as the living great apes—orangutan, gorilla, and

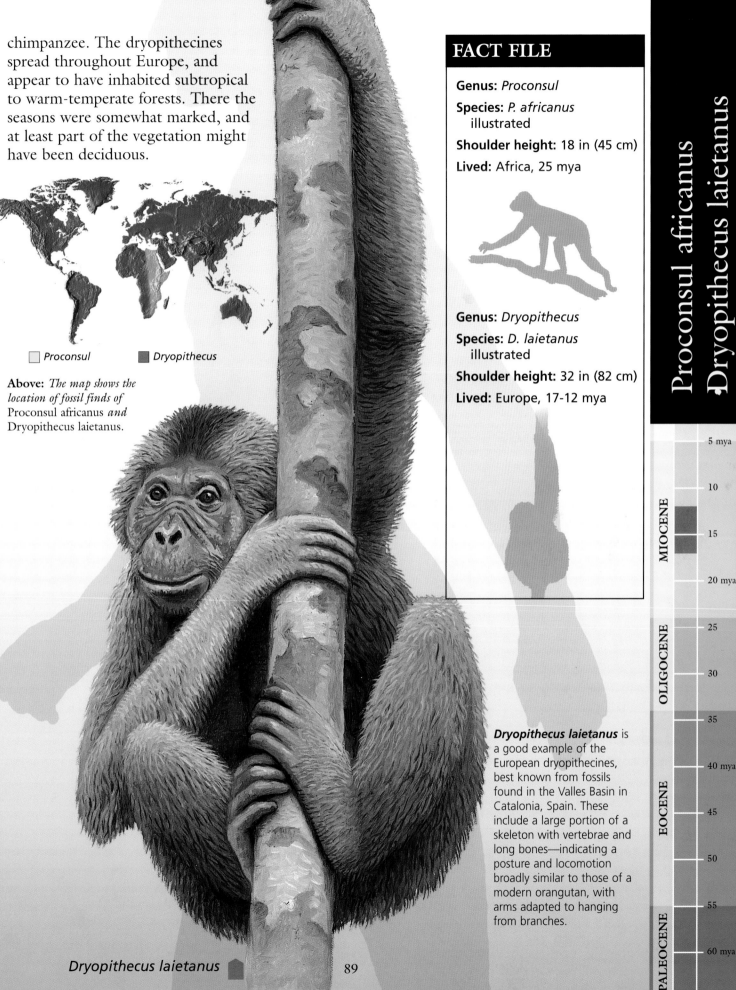

chimpanzee. The dryopithecines spread throughout Europe, and appear to have inhabited subtropical to warm-temperate forests. There the seasons were somewhat marked, and at least part of the vegetation might have been deciduous.

☐ *Proconsul*   ■ *Dryopithecus*

Above: *The map shows the location of fossil finds of* Proconsul africanus *and* Dryopithecus laietanus.

FACT FILE

Genus: *Proconsul*

Species: *P. africanus* illustrated

Shoulder height: 18 in (45 cm)

Lived: Africa, 25 mya

Genus: *Dryopithecus*

Species: *D. laietanus* illustrated

Shoulder height: 32 in (82 cm)

Lived: Europe, 17-12 mya

Proconsul africanus
Dryopithecus laietanus

Dryopithecus laietanus is a good example of the European dryopithecines, best known from fossils found in the Valles Basin in Catalonia, Spain. These include a large portion of a skeleton with vertebrae and long bones—indicating a posture and locomotion broadly similar to those of a modern orangutan, with arms adapted to hanging from branches.

Dryopithecus laietanus

89

MIOCENE

OLIGOCENE

EOCENE

PALEOCENE

5 mya
10
15
20 mya
25
30
35
40 mya
45
50
55
60 mya
65

Australopithecines

The australopithecines are an important part of the story of human evolution. But it is a complicated tale, made more so by new fossil discoveries.

Australopithecus afarensis and **A. africanus**
A. africanus was a small animal that walked erect, with the hands thus free to hold and carry. As with primates in general and many other mammals, males and females differered in size. Males might have weighed up to 90 lb (40 kg) and stood around 4 ft 3 in (1.3 m) tall, females 30-50 percent less. A. afarensis was broadly similar to A. africanus, but retained rather more primitive features. It was heavier and taller, with large males weighing up to 100 pounds (45 kg) and standing perhaps 5 feet (1.5 m). Although it was clearly an upright, bipedal walker, it probably retained more climbing ability than A. africanus.

Below: *A side view of a skull of an* Australopithecus africanus *child (from Taung, Cape Province), with a natural cast of the inside of the missing skull vault.*

The tree of human and ape evolution has many branches. One of the most important sprouted about 6 million years ago, when the African great apes went one way and another branch gave rise to the Hominini, or hominins—humans and their close relatives. This branch forks many times and the exact relationships of the creatures on it are difficult to work out. But because we have great interest in our own origins, scientists continue their search for more evidence. New discoveries are often made, so any account must be of work in progress.

In 1925, the skull of an apelike child was found in a quarry in Taung, South Africa. But the rounded shape of its forehead and the form of its teeth led the anatomist Raymond Dart to conclude that it was more like a human than an ape. Many other scientists disputed this at first.

But further finds in South Africa, mainly of skulls and teeth, confirmed Dart's view, and *Australopithecus africanus* was accepted as a plausible human ancestor.

The australopithecines—the name means "southern apes"—walked upright, like humans. Their brains were only about half the size of ours, but their bodies were much smaller. So the brain-to-bodyweight ratio was greater than that of the apes.

For many years, A. africanus was thought to be an ancestor of later human species, including our own. But more recent discoveries, together with more accurate dating of finds, have discredited this theory. One of the most important finds was of another, earlier species, A. afarensis, discovered in the late 1970s in Ethiopia and Tanzania. This seemed a more likely human ancestor. But now this in turn is in dispute as other species such as *Kenyanthropus platyops* have been put forward. So the debate goes on.

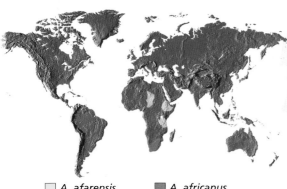

Left: *Known distributions of* A. afarensis *and* A. africanus.

Below: *Skeleton and life reconstruction of a female* Australopithecus africanus, *based on specimens from Sterkfontein, in South Africa.*

FACT FILE

Genus: *Australopithecus*

Species: *A. afarensis* and *A. africanus* illustrated

Height: 4 ft 3 in to 5 ft (1.3-1.5 m)

Lived: Africa, 3.9-2 mya

☐ *A. afarensis*　　■ *A. africanus*

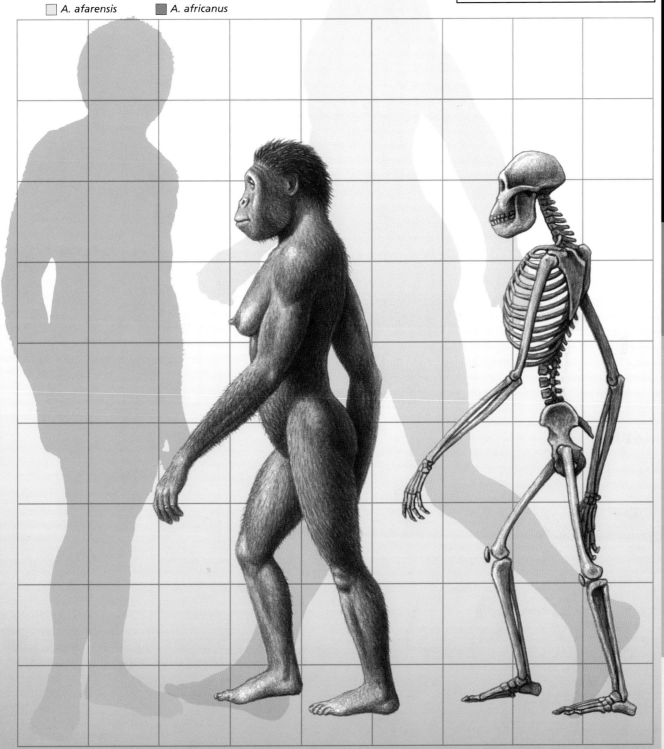

Australopithecus afarensis
Australopithecus africanus

HOLOCENE	present
	2,000 ya
	4,000 ya
	6,000 ya
	8,000 ya
	10,000 ya
	0.2 mya
	0.4
	0.6
PLEISTOCENE	0.8
	1 mya
	1.2
	1.4
	1.6
	1.8
	2 mya
PLIOCENE	3
	4
	5

A. afarensis ⬜　　*A. africanus* ⬛　　91

Australopithecines

The climbing ability of Australopithecus africanus might have been put to good use during late Pliocene encounters with large predators such as the saber-toothed cat Homotherium.

Paranthropus

Members of the genus Paranthropus *made up a side branch of the human family tree. They flourished in Africa from the late Pliocene to the mid-Pleistocene epoch.*

Above: *A skull of* Paranthropus boisei *from Olduvai Gorge in Tanzania found in 1959 shows the enormous cheek teeth.*

Paranthropus boisei and **Paranthropus robustus,** found respectively in eastern Africa and South Africa, between them show the typical features of the robust australopithecines. The skeleton is that of an upright, bipedal animal, and the hands suggest a precision grip and capable manipulation of small objects. The most prominent feature is the robust facial construction with massive brow ridges. This is matched by large cheek teeth, with strong muscles to provide the forces necessary for chewing.

Right *A skull of* Paranthropus robustus *from Swartkrans in South Africa.*

One group of hominins that are clearly not on a direct line to modern humans are the members of the genus *Paranthropus*. These were discovered during the 1930s in South Africa, and were at first considered to be a new species of *Australopithecus* (see pages 90-91). At that time, they were often referred to as the "robust" australopithecines to distinguish them informally from the less rugged *A. afarensis* and *A. africanus,* and the name has rather stuck. They were upright, bipedal animals, but the term robust refers to the size of the teeth and skull rather than to their build.

The two species

The robusts are known from distinct areas of Africa. *Paranthropus robustus,* the first to be found, is from southern Africa. It is known from the South African sites of Kromdraai, Swartkrans, and more recently Drimolen, where exceptionally good skull remains were found in the late 1990s. *Paranthropus boisei* is known from eastern Africa, and in particular from the famous locality of Olduvai Gorge. It was somewhat larger than its southern African relative, with males perhaps weighing up to 110 pounds (50 kg).

All robusts have large cheek teeth. Patterns on these of wear and damage suggest a hard and abrasive diet. There is also evidence on the skull of the attachment of large chewing muscles.

A different line

The specialized skull and dental features of the robusts suggest they were on a different evolutionary line from *Australopithecus,* and certainly from the one leading directly to our own genus, *Homo*. But they had brains of around the same size as the Australopithecines. Their huge teeth and their powerful jaw muscles suggest an emphasis on dealing with hard foodstuffs such as grains and nuts, or the grit involved in digging up tubers. But it is not known whether they also had tools to assist them in processing such food items.

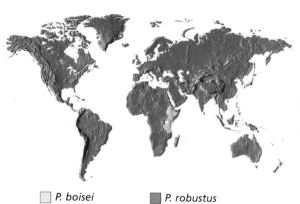

Left: *The areas in Africa where* Paranthropus *fossils have been found.*

Below: *The* boisei *species (left) was larger than* robustus *(right), but in any case females were considerably smaller than males in both species.*

☐ *P. boisei* ■ *P. robustus*

FACT FILE

Genus: *Paranthropus*

Species: *P. boisei* and *P. robustus*

Height: *P. boisei* 4 ft 6 in (1.4 m), *P. robustus* 4 ft 4 in (1.3 m)

Lived: Eastern and southern Africa, 2.5–1 mya

P. boisei male ☐ 95 *P. robustus female* ▮

HOLOCENE	present
	2,000 ya
	4,000 ya
	6,000 ya
	8,000 ya
	10,000 ya
	0.2 mya
	0.4
	0.6
PLEISTOCENE	0.8
	1 mya
	1.2
	1.4
	1.6
	1.8
	2 mya
PLIOCENE	3
	4
	5

Homo erectus

Stockily built, with a heavy-browed head, Homo erectus *is our earliest clear ancestor*

Below: *Evidence from Zhoukoudian Cave, in China, suggests that* Homo erectus *had learned how to make fire.*

Homo erectus were the first hominins to really look like modern human beings, although the heavy brow ridges and jaws might have made them unattractive to modern eyes. They were clever enough to make a wide range of implements, enabling them to dismember and process prey carcasses. They are known to have been scavengers, but whether they were active hunters is unclear.

Right: *A cast of the skull of* Homo erectus *from 1.8-million-year-old deposits at Koobi Fora, Kenya.*

Homo erectus is our earliest clear ancestor and shares our generic name, *Homo*. Bones were first discovered in the late 1800s in Java, Southeast Asia, then in caves near Beijing, China. These remains—hailed as a missing link between apes and modern humans—were less than a million years old. But more recent discoveries in eastern Africa and from Dmanisi in Georgia have pushed the age of this species back to about 1.8 million years. And further, unconfirmed finds in Java claim fossils only 25,000 years old.

Most early hominin remains consist of teeth and fragments of skulls. But in 1984, near Lake Turkana, in Kenya, the first pieces of bone were found, which proved to be an almost complete skeleton of a young *Homo erectus* boy. He was about 5 feet 4 inches (1.6 m) tall, but more strongly built than any modern boy, with a heavier face but a brain only two-thirds the size. He walked upright, and was probably already able to make and use the stone hand axes that were part of the advanced technology of his people. It was doubtless these that helped in the success of *Homo erectus,* as generation by generation they migrated on the long, hard journeys that took them eventually from Africa across both Europe and Asia.

Tools and fire

Homo erectus made and used a variety of stone tools that differed little across their wide range. We know more about the distribution of the species from finds of tools than from their rare remains. And there is evidence also of another major advance in technology. The site at Zhoukoudian, near Beijing, shows that some *Homo erectus* populations had learned the use of fire—one of mankind's greatest tools.

Left: *The major fossil finds of* Homo erectus—*in Africa, Georgia, China, and Java (Indonesia).*

FACT FILE

Genus: *Homo*

Species: *H. erectus*

Height: up to 5 ft 11 in (1.8 m)

Lived: Africa and Eurasia, 1.8 mya-*25,000 ya
* unconfirmed

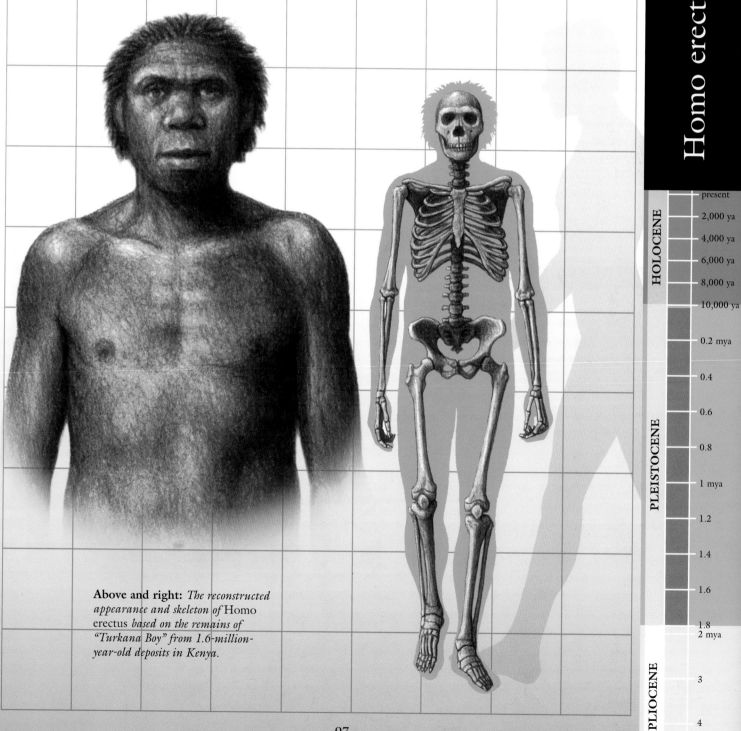

Above and right: *The reconstructed appearance and skeleton of* Homo erectus *based on the remains of "Turkana Boy" from 1.6-million-year-old deposits in Kenya.*

Homo erectus

HOLOCENE	present
	2,000 ya
	4,000 ya
	6,000 ya
	8,000 ya
	10,000 ya
	0.2 mya
	0.4
	0.6
PLEISTOCENE	0.8
	1 mya
	1.2
	1.4
	1.6
	1.8
	2 mya
PLIOCENE	3
	4
	5

Homo antecessor

Based on fragments of several individuals found in northern Spain, Homo antecessor *is claimed to be the oldest human species known from Europe.*

Below: *The head of one of the Atapuerca specimens, a boy of 11 or 12 years, reconstructed from fragments. The muscles, which are placed according to markings on the bone, give the general shape to the face, although the size of the ears can only be estimated.*

Fragments of skull and other bones from at least six individuals of various ages provide evidence of when *H. antecessor* lived. The rock deposits from which the material comes—level TD6 in the area of the site known as Gran Dolina, at Atapuerca, Spain— places them earlier than 780,000 years ago. The species name, *antecessor*, given to mark this early date, derives from that given to advance troops of the ancient Roman legions.

The skull material suggests that *H. antecessor* had a relatively modern looking face, but with a fairly primitive forehead region. However, the volume of the adult skull suggests a brain approaching the bottom end of the range for modern humans. This combination of features differs from that of African representatives of *Homo erectus*, and has led the Spanish researchers to argue that *H. antecessor* is the last common ancestor of both modern humans and the Neandertals.

Stages of reconstruction (from the left)

Complete skull   Muscles   Features

98

In this scheme, the Neandertals descended from an African group of *H. antecessor* via populations represented in Europe by a variety of fossils. These include those of later deposits at Atapuerca and also from the sites of Mauer and Steinheim in Germany and Swanscombe in England. Likewise, the Spanish researchers argue, fully modern humans might have descended from an African group of *H. antecessor* via populations represented by African fossils.

Possible cannibalism

With the human material at Atapuerca are numerous examples of worked stone. This indicates some form of activity at the site. But most intriguing of all, several of the human bones show traces of cut marks that suggest these earliest of Europeans might have practiced cannibalism.

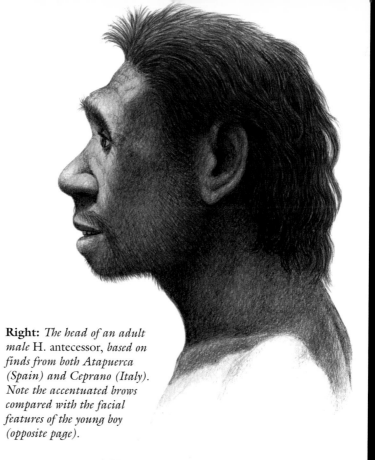

Right: *The head of an adult male* H. antecessor, *based on finds from both Atapuerca (Spain) and Ceprano (Italy). Note the accentuated brows compared with the facial features of the young boy (opposite page).*

● **Finds of *Homo antecessor***

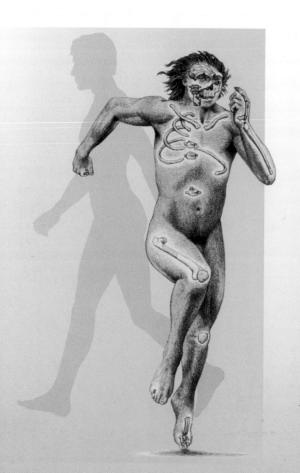

Above: *Bones of* H. antecessor *from at least six individuals were found at Atapuerca, Spain, in 1994. There is still debate about whether later finds in Italy may be attributed to the same species.*

Left: *A generalized reconstruction of the life appearance of the TD6* Homo antecessor *based on the various skeletal parts recovered. Although the head and face are relatively primitive in appearance, the body and limbs might have looked more like those of a living person.*

FACT FILE

Genus: *Homo*

Species: *H. antecessor*

Height: Uncertain, possibly about 5 ft 8 in (1.73 m)

Lived: Southern Europe, more than 780,000 ya

HOLOCENE
present
2,000 ya
4,000 ya
6,000 ya
8,000 ya
10,000 ya
0.2 mya
0.4
0.6

PLEISTOCENE
0.8
1 mya
1.2
1.4
1.6
1.8
2 mya

PLIOCENE
3
4
5

Neandertals

Perhaps the best known of all our fossil relatives are the Neandertals, rugged creatures but with surprisingly large brains and a wide range of stone tools.

Homo neanderthalensis
Individuals were strongly built with relatively short shins. The skeleton bears all the hallmarks of a hard life. Their stone tools suggest a range of activities centered on processing animal carcasses, probably for clothing as well as food.

The Neandertals, the best known of all our fossil relatives, evolved from the original human dispersal to Europe. Their name comes from a discovery in the Neander Valley in Germany in 1856. Ideas about their place in human evolution have varied, but most experts now see them as a distinct species, *Homo neanderthalensis*.

Through numerous discoveries in western Europe and the Middle East, they are one of the best studied hominin species. They were strong creatures used to a physically hard life, but not the shambling brutes of many early reconstructions. Their skull was long and low, with a large nasal opening. Their brow ridges were massive, and the face and jaws projected. But they had large brains averaging slightly above our own in size, and they used a wide range of stone implements, from hand axes to hammer stones.

Whether they had speech as we would recognize it is unknown. But the level of social organization required to make that range of tools and to live in such harsh conditions suggests good communication and at least some language ability.

Above: *The known distribution of Neandertal remains includes Europe and Asia east to Uzbekistan.*

Below: *The Neandertal cranium from Forbes Quarry, Gibraltar, found in 1848.*

Homo neanderthalensis

FACT FILE

Genus: *Homo*

Species:
 H. neanderthalensis

Height: 5 ft 5 in (1.7 m)

Lived: Europe, Asia east to Uzbekistan, 200,000-30,000 ya

Homo sapiens

All living humans belong to the same species, Homo sapiens, *which originated in Africa and has become one of the most successful to have occupied the planet.*

Homo sapiens originated in Africa. The oldest known specimen comes from Ethiopia and dates back some 160,000 years. In Europe, *H. sapiens* appeared to have replaced the Neandertals by about 30,000 years ago. Whether the process was natural or not is unknown. Other parts of the world were occupied at different rates. *Homo sapiens* spread

to Asia and Australia at least as early as to Europe, although northeastern Asia was a little later. The New World, the Americas, was last of all at no more than 15,000 to 12,000 years ago.

The appearance of *Homo sapiens* is marked not only by a new body plan, but also by a greater range of ever more sophisticated tools and tool kits and the eventual appearance of decorative arts. In its later stages, our fossil record is accompanied by increasingly detailed evidence of developments in technology and social behavior.

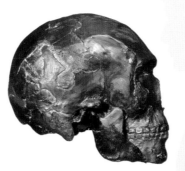

Above: *A reconstruction of a 130,000-year-old skull of* Homo sapiens *from Ethiopia.*

Left: Homo sapiens *originated in Africa, where the oldest known specimen, from 160,000 years ago, was found in Ethiopia.*

Homo sapiens fossils differ from Neandertals' in having long and slender limbs, a high forehead, and a more rounded cranial vault containing the brain. The face is relatively small, with a well-developed chin. *H. sapiens* was the first hominin species to attain a world-wide distribution, a feat aided by its intelligence, cooperative strategies, and increasingly sophisticated technological abilities.

FACT FILE

Genus: *Homo*

Species: *H. sapiens*

Height: Varies greatly

Lived: Worldwide, from 160,000 ya

Homo sapiens

HOLOCENE	present
	2,000 ya
	4,000 ya
	6,000 ya
	8,000 ya
	10,000 ya
	0.2 mya
	0.4
	0.6
PLEISTOCENE	0.8
	1 mya
	1.2
	1.4
	1.6
	1.8
	2 mya
PLIOCENE	3
	4
	5

Insectivores

Many animals eat insects, an abundant and nutritious source of food. Most early mammals probably included them in their diet or existed largely on them.

Leptictidium nasutum is known in great detail from the middle Eocene shale deposits at Messel in Germany, where stomach contents have even been recovered. Although not formally classified in the Insectivora, it appears to have been an insectivore-like animal—rather like a large elephant shrew with an elongated snout, but with even more elongated rear legs. But unlike other small mammals with such extended rear legs, it does not appear to have been especially well adapted for jumping or hopping. It might have been more of a bipedal (two-legged) runner.

Insects are abundant in many habitats, and they provide a rich meal for any animal that specializes in their capture. The term "insectivore" simply means "eater of insects." It is probably a fair description of many early mammals, based on their size and the type of teeth they had. And we know there were insects around for them to eat, because their remains can survive extremely well in some deposits. *Leptictidium nasutum* (below) was one such insectivorous creature. But what we may term true insectivores are members of the order Insectivora. And that name we reserve for animals such as the living hedgehogs, shrews, and moles. A variety of fossil species may also be placed in this formal group, which is known probably from the late Cretaceous (85 mya).

Patchy fossil record

Members of the Insectivora are generally rather primitive in form. They are small animals that retain a full set of teeth that enable them to deal with the tough carapace (shell) of insects. Like other small mammals, insectivores have a patchy fossil record. Those that are found tend to come from deposits where exceptional preservation processes

Leptictidium nasutum

occurred, such as rapid burial in soft sediments. A particularly good example of this may be seen at the German Eocene site of Messel (see page 105), where true, hedgehoglike insectivores occur together with *Leptictidium*. The deposits there also contain the remains of a rich variety of insects, including giant ants and numerous beetles.

Some of the fossil species were also much larger than their living relatives, and this might have helped to ensure that their skeletons were found. *Deinogalerix koenigswaldi* (below), a hairy hedgehog, was one such animal—similar in size to a domestic cat and presumably rather more aggressive in its behavior.

Deinogalerix koenigswaldi was similar to modern hairy hedgehogs, or moonrats, but with a relatively longer snout. It was around the size of a domestic cat. It is known from late Miocene deposits in eastern Italy. Like its modern relatives, it was probably omnivorous. Its size, limbs, and teeth indicate it probably obtained its food by scavenging.

Below: *A cast of a skull of* Deinogalerix koenigswaldi *shows the elongated snout and many teeth of a typical insect eater.*

Deinogalerix koenigswaldi

5 mya

10

MIOCENE

15

20 mya

25

OLIGOCENE

30

35

40 mya

EOCENE

45

50

55

PALEOCENE

60 mya

65

Bats

With about 1,000 living species, bats are second only to rodents in diversity among mammals. Even the oldest known fossil bats show little difference from bats of today.

Icaronycteris, a small microchiropteran from early Eocene deposits in Wyoming, is the oldest known bat. Skeletally, it is little different from a modern bat, with long front limbs and extended fingers. This clearly shows that the full anatomical specializations of the bats had developed by this time.

The huge and diverse array of living bats is divided into two suborders, the large fruit-eating species of the Megachiroptera and the smaller, more numerous and usually insect-eating Microchiroptera. Insect-eating, or insectivorous, bats are widely distributed and occur in vast numbers. Fruit bats are more restricted in habitat requirements and therefore less widely found. Almost all microchiropteran bats rely to some extent on echolocation of prey—hence the often large ears and strange, fleshy nasal structures in many species. These structures are used in detection, although some employ more passive sound location. A small number of microchiropterans eat fruits, and these use smell and vision in location of food.

Specialized for flight

As the only flying mammals, bats have exceptionally thin, lightweight, and extremely fragile bones. They are therefore rare as fossils unless some process has concentrated their remains. One of the best early examples is that of *Icaronycteris index* from early Eocene deposits in North America. And although it is represented by only a handful of specimens, *Icaronycteris* shows clearly a

Icaronycteris

skeleton little different from that of a living bat. In other words, the earliest specimens have a highly evolved and specialized skeleton. This implies a much longer evolutionary history than we actually see in the sparse record. Many authorities suspect an original link with insectivores, although this may prove hard to establish on the basis of fossil finds.

Archaeopteropus, from the Oligocene of Italy, had a wingspan of 32 in (82 cm). It has been classified as a megachiropteran bat, although some authorities believe that it was simply a large microchiropteran. The difference is not merely academic—its allocation to the Megachiroptera implies an earlier origin for the fruit bats.

FACT FILE

Genus: *Icaronycteris*
Wingspan: 11.5 in (29 cm)
Lived: North America, 52-50 mya

Genus: *Archaeopteropus*
Wingspan: 32 in (82 cm)
Lived: Italy, 31-28 mya

Genus: *Palaeochiropteryx*
Wingspan: 10 in (25 cm)
Lived: Germany, 50-48 mya

Archaeopteropus   10 in (25 cm)

Messel fossils

Numerous spectacularly complete bat fossils are known from the middle Eocene deposits at Messel, Germany. Preserved from an ancient lake and found in an abandoned mine pit, they cover a range of genera. Many specimens show fur, and some even have stomach contents of identifiable bits of moths. So we know, for example, that the bats were definitely nocturnal, because their diet consisted of nocturnal prey.

Palaeochiropteryx, a microchiropteran from Messel, had the wing proportions of a low-level flier able to maneuver within the forest canopy and catch insects near the water surface. Death during such flights, perhaps as a result of suffocation in gases given off by the lake sediments, may be why so many complete specimens were preserved at the site.

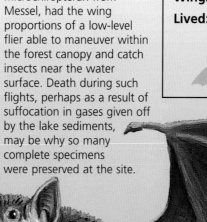

5 mya	
10	MIOCENE
15	
20 mya	
25	OLIGOCENE
30	
35	
40 mya	EOCENE
45	
50	
55	
60 mya	PALEOCENE
65	

Bats

A scene in the middle Miocene rain forest at Messel, Germany: The bats Palaeochiropteryx (bottom left) and Hassianycteris (top right) fly among the trees, while the early carnivore Paroodectes (right) hunts Peradectes, a small marsupial

Creodonts

The creodonts were the dominant and largest land-based meat-eaters until the emergence of true carnivores, such as dogs and cats.

Machaeroides eothen
lived in the Eocene epoch in the Bridger Basin of North America. It was among the smallest members of the family Hyaenodontidae, but had saber teeth like those seen in several families of true carnivores. Since it was not much bigger than a domestic cat, these teeth were clearly not for dealing with large prey.

Below: Proviverra, *a small hyaenodont, is depicted in the early Eocene in a forest at La Boixedat, in the Spanish Pyrenees.*

The creodonts are all now extinct. They were carnivores, but formed a separate order from the living Carnivora (the "true" carnivores such as dogs, bears, and cats). Creodonts were predators or scavengers, and spanned the range of sizes and types found in the living order. They were the dominant carnivores of the world for tens of millions of years. The order, called the Creodonta, contained two families—the Oxyaenidae and the Hyaenodontidae.

The Oxyaenidae, although known from Asia, lived mainly in North America, in a range of catlike to weasel-like forms. Hyaenodonts,

members of the family Hyaenodontidae, had a wider distribution, reaching North America, Eurasia, and Africa. In Africa they evolved into gigantic forms, one of which, *Hyainailouros sulzeri,* eventually colonized Europe. Hyaenodonts looked like dogs with a big head. Their teeth were adapted to a mixed diet of meat and bone.

Difference lies in the teeth

Creodonts differed from the later, true carnivores in how their molars were modified for eating meat. In the Carnivora, the

Machaeroides eothen

upper fourth premolar and the lower first molar form the carnassials, or main slicing teeth. But in the creodonts, these were formed by the upper first or second molar and the lower second or third molar. This might seem a trivial difference, but to the experts it indicates a separate evolution. And that means a separate order. It is even possible that the creodonts themselves do not form a single natural group.

Hyainailouros sulzeri, a member of the family Hyaenodontidae, was a giant meat-eater. Its skull was 20 inches (50 cm) in length, and its body was long with short legs. Its teeth functioned as meat-slicers and bone-crushers. It was probably a good runner, but its feet, unlike those of cats, were not adapted for capturing prey. It might have been more of a scavenger. Hyenas of the time, members of the Carnivora, were small animals with teeth suggestive of insect-eaters. So they would have offered no competition.

Left: *This is a depiction of a scene at the late Eocene site of Roc de Santa, in Catalonia, Spain. A group of the hyaenodont* Hyaenodon *feed on a carcass of the horselike* Palaeotherium.

FACT FILE

Genus: *Machaeroides*
Species: *M. eothen* illustrated
Shoulder height: 10 in (25 cm)
Lived: North America, 47-42 mya

Genus: *Hyainailouros*
Species: *H. sulzeri* illustrated
Shoulder height: 35 in (90 cm)
Lived: Africa, Asia, Europe, 22-18 mya

Hyainailouros sulzeri

109

5 mya

MIOCENE

10

15

20 mya

OLIGOCENE

25

30

35

EOCENE

40 mya

45

50

55

PALEOCENE

60 mya

65

Bear-dogs

Some of the earliest larger members of the order Carnivora, or true carnivores, looked rather like a cross between a small bear and a large dog— hence the name "bear-dogs."

Amphicyon major, found in numerous European Miocene localities, had a mixture of features—a long, catlike back and tail, broad bearlike feet with claws that did not retract, and a doglike skull containing numerous teeth. It was large, with males probably reaching in excess of 400 lb (180 kg). And it might have been an active hunter, probably operating by ambushing its prey rather than by chasing.

The order Carnivora contains about 250 living species, and with everything from weasels to polar bears, it is one of the most diverse of the orders of mammals. The creodonts were the ruling predators in most parts of the world from about 60 million to 30 million years ago. But the Carnivora, insignificant creatures for some 30 million years, had begun to replace them near the end of the Eocene (about 35 mya). Among the earliest to make their mark were the amphicyonids, or bear-dogs, a family of superficially bearlike carnivores. Their fossils are most commonly found in North America, but are also known from Eurasia and Africa.

The name

The name bear-dog stems from the fact that the amphicyonids were previously included with the family Canidae, the true dogs. Most taxonomists consider the bears and dogs, along with the mustelids (weasels) and raccoons, to be more closely related to each than to other members of the Carnivora.

Amphicyonids quickly diversified into a number of forms during the early Miocene (24-20 mya). Some were fast-moving, specialist meat-eaters. Others retained a more generalized and bearlike form and were perhaps scavengers. Still others might have resembled pandas. But all were agile predators. During the middle Miocene (about 10 mya), some of the smaller and the less specialized species declined. But the large European species *Amphicyon major* prospered and is widely known from many deposits.

Below: *In a wooded part of Spain during the early Miocene, a group of bear-dogs drag a pig carcass to a less open site for consumption. In the background a pair of Ampelomeryx, members of an extinct family of horned herbivores, continue to eat the vegetation and are undisturbed by the spectacle.*

FACT FILE

Genus: *Amphicyon*

Species: *A. major* illustrated

Head/body length: 5 ft 6 in (1.7 m)

Lived: Europe, 15-12 mya

MIOCENE	5 mya
	10
	15
	20 mya
OLIGOCENE	25
	30
	35
EOCENE	40 mya
	45
	50
	55
PALEOCENE	60 mya
	65

Dogs

The dogs, or canids, with some 35 living species worldwide, are divided into one living subfamily and two fossil subfamilies. One of the latter, the borophagines, produced the biggest dogs ever.

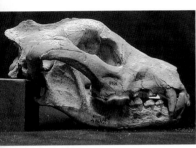

Above: *The massive skull of the borophagine dog* Epicyon saevus.

Below: *A small raccoon dog of the living genus* Nyctereutes *that lived in Europe from 3 to 1 mya.*

Hesperocyon gregarius is an early dog from the later Eocene and the Oligocene epochs of North America. Like all earliest dogs, it was a small animal, perhaps the size of a fox. With its elongated body and neck, it looked more like a civet than a dog. Such animals would probably have lived in a community and hunted small animals by stalking and pouncing rather than by chasing for any distance.

The first dogs were the hesperocyonines. These emerged in North America about 40 million years ago and survived there for some 30 million years. They were essentially small animals and came in a variety of forms. But some of the later species in the subfamily weighed up to perhaps 44 pounds (20 kg). By this time, the borophagine dogs were present in the form of the giant *Epicyon* genus.

The borophagine dogs were the second major group of the canid family to establish themselves. Like the hesperocyonines, they were also successful in North America for a long period and in a number of forms. They eventually became extinct about 2 million years ago.

Some of the borophagines were giants among dogs—*Epicyon haydeni*

was larger than any member of the modern-day dog family. They are often characterized as bone-eating animals. Various species showed a variety of adaptations, but the ability to crush bone was only one of these. Indeed this speciality, which calls for powerful teeth, was confined in its extreme form to later and smaller members

□ Hesperocyon ■ Epicyon

Left: *The two major dog subfamilies, the hesperocyonines and the borophagines, were confined to North America. The living dog family also originated there, and spread to the rest of the world about 3 mya.*

of the group. Among these were species of the genus *Borophagus*, which means "bone eater"—hence the name of the subfamily. Unlike in hyenas, where the largest species have been the specialized bone-crunchers, the development of cone-shaped teeth—a major requirement for bone-eating—was not very advanced in the borophagines.

Epicyon haydeni The genus *Epicyon* included probably the largest and most impressive of the dogs over their long period of evolution. *E. haydeni* even reached the height of a small lion. Although it might not have been able to crack bone to the extent that its sheer size would suggest, it was certainly a powerful predator.

FACT FILE

Genus: *Hesperocyon*

Species: *H. gregarius* illustrated

Shoulder height: 8 in (20 cm)

Lived: North America, 37-29 mya

Genus: *Epicyon*

Species: *E. haydeni* illustrated

Shoulder height: 37 in (95 cm)

Lived: North America, 12-5 mya

MIOCENE	5 mya
	10
	15
	20 mya
OLIGOCENE	25
	30
	35
EOCENE	40 mya
	45
	50
PALEOCENE	55
	60 mya
	65

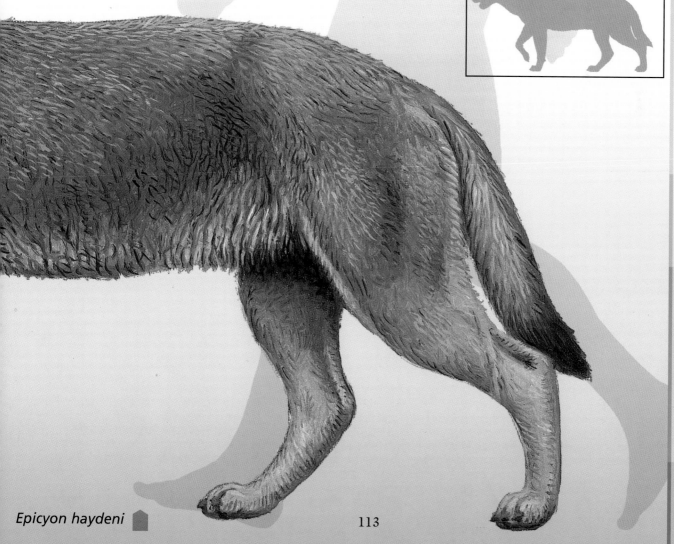

Epicyon haydeni ▮

Dogs

Two borophagine dogs of the species Aelurodon ferox have prey in sight as they move through woodland in middle Miocene North America. Wolf-size animals, these predators had teeth indicating a wolflike diet

Bears

Bears have a long evolutionary history, dating back nearly 25 million years. Some of the fossil species were bigger even than today's grizzlies or polar bears.

Arctodus simus, known as the short-faced bear, was a large and impressive predator. Besides its shortened face, it had a shortened body and longer limbs than a typical bear. This would suggest it was faster moving and perhaps a more aggressive predator than most living species. Its great size placed it above the saber-toothed cats *Smilodon* and *Homotherium* in the hierarchy of predators. It was even larger than the enormous American lions of the period.

Bears belong to the family Ursidae. Today there are some eight species, all large animals, although the enormous polar and brown bears dominate the size range. Large size means that bears have a generally good fossil record, which dates from earliest Miocene times (24 mya) onward. And although over that period actual sizes have varied considerably, some of the fossil forms were bigger than even the most impressive of living relatives.

Bears are not well adapted to run fast over a distance. Although they are members of the order Carnivora, many living species could more properly be described as omnivores, able to subsist on a varied diet of plants and animals. Only the polar bear, with few plants in its habitat, is almost entirely a carnivore.

Plant-eaters and predators

It would seem that, in general, fossil species also had omnivorous tendencies. Some, such as the huge European cave bear, *Ursus spelaeus,* show this to a marked degree, with large, flat teeth well suited to grinding.

Arctodus simus   116

But others among the fossil species were clearly very active predators. Early forms with predatory features include the European species *Hemicyon sansaniensis,* known from early Miocene deposits at Sansan in France. Its body structure was more like a pursuit predator such as a dog. But the most extreme of the predatory bears was the North American giant short-faced bear, *Arctodus simus,* an animal standing perhaps 5 feet (1.5 m) at the shoulder.

Ursus spelaeus, the cave bear, is known in spectacular numbers running into thousands of individuals in cave deposits of the last ice age in Europe. Its domed forehead and deep mandible (lower jaw) gave extra space for muscles used in chewing. They drove the grinding function of the large and flattened molar teeth.

Above: *The skull of a European cave bear,* Ursus spelaeus, *showing the typically high forehead of this species.*

Left: *The map highlights the distribution of the featured bears in North America and Eurasia.*

☐ *Arctodus simus*   ■ *Ursus spelaeus*

FACT FILE

Genus: *Arctodus*

Species: *A. simus* illustrated

Shoulder height: 5 ft (1.5 m)

Lived: North America, 1.5 mya–10,000 ya

Genus: *Ursus*

Species: *U. spelaeus* illustrated

Shoulder height: 4 ft (1.2 m)

Lived: Europe and western Asia, 300,000–10,000 ya

Arctodus simus
Ursus spelaeus

present
2,000 ya
4,000 ya
6,000 ya
8,000 ya
10,000 ya

HOLOCENE

0.2 mya
0.4
0.6
0.8
1 mya
1.2
1.4
1.6
1.8
2 mya

PLEISTOCENE

3
4
5

Ursus spelaeus

117

Seals and relatives

Seals, sea lions, and walruses are carnivores that live in water. The fossil record shows how they evolved from land animals.

Enaliarctos mealsi is one of the oldest sea-lion-like animals known. Though it had legs much like those of land animals, it is likely that its toes were webbed. Its skull shows us that it had very big eyes and the nerve supply for huge whiskers, like those of modern sea lions. It probably lived somewhat like a sea otter, but its teeth suggest that it fed on many foods, including fish.

Seals, sea lions, and walruses are known collectively as the Pinnipedia, a name that means "fin-footed." They spend most of their life in the sea, but they can haul ashore to rest or produce their young. The fossil record, though far from complete, shows that the group we know as the true seals might have descended from an otterlike creature, while the so-called eared seals and the walrus probably evolved from ancestors more like dogs or bears.

True seals move differently from the other members of the group. Their hind legs have turned backward to make very efficient paddles, though on land they cannot be used to bear any weight. They are the most widespread group, living from the tropics to polar regions. The best clue to their evolution is a Miocene fossil from France called *Potamotherium*, which looked like a cross between an otter and a seal. At about the same time, on the coast of what is now California, an almost bearlike animal called *Enaliarctos* already had some of the characteristics of sea lions of today. By the late Miocene, animals much like today's sea lions had evolved. From ancestors like *Enaliarctos,* several walruslike animals with small tusks had evolved by early Pliocene times.

FACT FILE

Genus: *Enaliarctos*

Species: *E. mealsi* illustrated

Length: 7 ft (2 m)

Lived: Western North America, 23-16 mya

Enaliarctos mealsi

Mustelids

Living mustelids range in size from tiny weasels up to large otters. But at least one fossil species was the size of a leopard.

The family Mustelidae includes animals such as mink, skunks, otters, and badgers. They have longish bodies and short limbs, and range in size from the smallest weasels at an ounce or so (30 g) up to the South American giant otter at 70 pounds (32 kg). They have large numbers of teeth, and eat a variety of foods, including eggs, insects, and other small animals. Fish, crabs, and mollusks are staple foods of otters.

The record of mustelids goes back at least 25 million years. Fossil mustelids are extremely varied, although the larger species are best represented. Most of the fossil forms have the typical body plan seen in living species. But the large *Ekorus ekakeran* from late Miocene deposits in Kenya shows a trend toward a more catlike body.

Ekorus ekakeran, from 6 million-year-old deposits in Kenya, was, by mustelid standards, a gigantic creature. Its body and teeth, and presumably lifestyle, were more like that of a cat the size of a leopard. The longer legs in particular suggest that it might have been a fast runner. The teeth are those of a meat-eater, but show no evidence of bone-crunching ability.

Right: *The small mustelid* Plesictis *in pursuit of a small rodent. Such mustelids are known from Oligocene times in Europe.*

FACT FILE

Genus: *Ekorus*

Species: *E. ekakeran* illustrated

Shoulder height: 24 in (60 cm)

Lived: Eastern Africa, 6 mya

Ekorus ekakeran

PLIOCENE	1.8 2 mya
	3
	4
	5 mya
MIOCENE	10
	15
	20 mya
OLIGOCENE	25
	30
	35
EOCENE	40 mya
	45

Nimravids

Long before cats appeared, a group of catlike animals, the nimravids, lived much like them. The saber-toothed species are referred to as false saber-tooths to distinguish them from true cats.

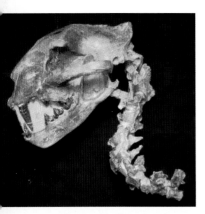

Above: *Skull and neck vertebrae of the nimravid* Nimravus brachiops. *This animal was about the size of a large lynx.*

Right: *The nimravid* Hoplophoneus mentalis *lived in western North America.*

Hoplophoneus mentalis, a false saber-tooth from western North America, had impressively elongated upper canines. It was the size of a small leopard, but with shorter, more robust legs. It walked more on the soles of its feet than on its toes.

The nimravids are an extinct group of animals very similar in many features to the cats. They were previously thought to belong to the cat family, the Felidae, but most paleontologists now place them in a separate family. Their retractable claws, well-developed canine teeth, and slicing cheek teeth indicate very similar lifestyles to the cats. This would have been seen in particular in their hunting techniques and prey-handling methods. Nimravids were quite varied but, unlike the true cats, all appear to have had bladelike upper canines. In this feature they showed an even greater tendency toward the development of saber-toothed upper canines.

Pick of the prey

Animals such as *Hoplophoneus mentalis* would take prey as large as or larger than themselves. Prey might have included primitive horses, early camels, and a variety of oreodonts, members of a wholly extinct family of even-toed, sheeplike to piglike ungulates. Unlike dogs and hyenas, which can tackle animals only with their teeth, nimravids could seize their prey using their claws. But their role as the main predators of this kind appears to have been taken over by the true cats from mid-Miocene time (15 mya) onward.

FACT FILE

Genus: *Hoplophoneus*

Species: *H. mentalis* illustrated

Shoulder height: 19 in (48 cm)

Lived: Western North America, 35–29 mya

Hoplophoneus mentalis

Civets

Civets belong to the mongoose family. Most living civets are small, graceful animals. But some of their ancestors were much larger, and their cutting teeth were better adapted to make them more active predators.

Civets, together with mongooses, belong to the family Viverridae, a group of slender, long-bodied, somewhat catlike animals. Viverrids are extremely diverse, with some 70 living species occupying a range of habitats. Some move easily through the trees and are often thought to offer a good idea of what a primitive true carnivore would have looked like. Viverrids are thought to be related to cats, and in fact the fossa—a Madagascan viverrid—has a skeleton that resembles that of the earliest known cat, *Proailurus*.

Most civets are small animals, weighing no more than 5-6 pounds (2–3 kg), although the African civet can weigh up to 44 pounds (20 kg). Their fossil history is patchy, but a large species, *Viverra leakeyi*, has been identified from fossil specimens in Tanzania, South Africa, and Morocco.

Viverra leakeyi was similar in shape to modern ground civets of the Asiatic genus *Viverra*, but much larger— about the size of a jackal. The teeth were more adapted to cutting meat than those of modern members of the genus or the closely related African civet. This feature suggests that *V. leakeyi* was more of an active predator of small- and medium-size prey.

Below: *Remains of the large civet* Viverra leakeyi *have been found in Tanzania, South Africa, and Morocco.*

FACT FILE

Genus: *Viverra*
Species: *V. leakeyi*
Shoulder height: 16 in (40 cm)
Lived: Africa, about 5 mya

Viverra leakeyi

Hoplophoneus mentalis
Viverra leakeyi

5 mya

10

MIOCENE

15

20 mya

25

OLIGOCENE

30

35

40 mya

EOCENE

45

50

55

PALEO...

65

Cats

Members of the family Felidae, or felids, are all supreme predators. Cats occupy a wide range of habitats and their fossil record is good. Most extinct species were saber-tooths.

Cats are efficient predators, able to run, climb, and swim in pursuit of prey. Lions operate cooperatively, while most others hunt singly. The bigger species can tackle animals much larger than themselves. Cats seem to have originated in Eurasia, where the earliest known is a small animal named *Proailurus lemanensis*, found in French deposits of about 30 mya. It was about 16 inches (40 cm) high at the shoulder, with more teeth than living cats.

The 37 living species of wild cats are placed in three subfamilies of conical-toothed cats: the Pantherinae (including members of the genus *Panthera*, such as the lion), the Acinonychinae (the cheetah), and the Felinae (other cats). However, much

of the prehistoric family appears to be dominated by the saber-toothed cats of the subfamily Machairodontinae, belonging to genera such as *Dinofelis*, *Homotherium*, *Megantereon*, *Smilodon*, and *Xenosmilus*. They had very different characteristics from living cats.

Saber-tooths

Living cats can grip with their claws and bite into the neck or throat of their prey while still wrestling it to the ground. But the saber-toothed species could not have risked damage or breakage to their teeth in such a manner. Instead, they probably secured their prey on the ground first, positioning themselves behind the animal and bearing down with

Megantereon has been found widely in Africa and Eurasia, ranging even into North America, although the true number of species is unclear. The upper canine teeth were well developed and bladelike, and the forelimbs extremely muscular. The body proportions suggest a strong ambush predator, able to subdue struggling prey sufficiently to minimize damage to the teeth during the kill.

Megantereon cultridens

122

Dinofelis barlowi

their weight across the shoulders and chest. Only then did they administer a rapid, precisely aimed bite into the front of the throat, severing veins, arteries, and the windpipe. There would be no danger to the predator's canines of contact with any bone.

The saber-toothed cats would probably have hunted prey of their own body weight or less, such as small deer and antelope. Those that hunted in groups, such as some species of *Smilodon* and *Homotherium*, possibly tackled young mammoths.

Species of *Smilodon* and *Homotherium* are the most recent of the saber-toothed cats—they became extinct only 10,000 years ago, at the end of the last ice age. But for that accident of fate, they might still be with us.

Dinofelis This genus contains several species, the best examples of which are known from Africa, although it also ranged across Eurasia and into North America. These animals are often known as "false" saber-tooths, because the upper canines are less elongated and flattened than in other machairodonts. They appear to have been powerfully built, short-pursuit predators rather like modern jaguars.

Homotherium is known from Africa, Eurasia, and North America, and several species have been proposed. All had well-developed and flattened upper canines, and their strong incisors enabled them to pull muscle tissue from the bones of prey. The long front limbs suggest a cantering gait. These animals might have been pursuit predators—acting in groups to chase and bring down prey.

FACT FILE

Genus: *Megantereon*

Species: *M. cultridens* illustrated

Shoulder height: 28 in (70 cm)

Lived: In Africa, 3.0 to 1.5 mya, N. America, 3.2 to 1.6 mya Eurasia, 2.5 to 0.8 mya

---

Genus: *Dinofelis*

Species: *D. barlowi* illustrated

Shoulder height: 28 in (70 cm)

Lived: In Africa, 8-1.5 mya, N. America, 2.2 to 1.8 mya Eurasia, 4.5 to 1.5 mya

---

Genus: *Homotherium*

Species: *H. latidens* illustrated

Shoulder height: 44 in (110 cm)

Lived: In Africa, 5.0 to 1.5 mya N. America, 3.0 to 0.01 mya Eurasia, 3.0 to 0.5 mya

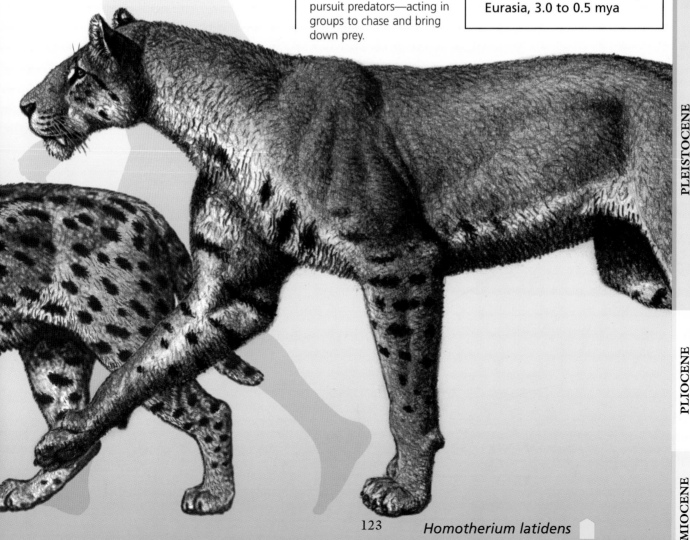

123   *Homotherium latidens*

PLEISTOCENE

PLIOCENE

MIOCENE

10,000 y.
0.2 mya
0.4
0.6
0.8
1 mya
1.2
1.4
1.6
1.8
2 mya
3
4
5
10
15

Xenosmilus

This cat, bigger than a lion, was discovered in 1981 in Florida deposits about 1 million years old. It had saber teeth similar to Homotherium and the compact body and short, powerful legs of Smilodon.

Smilodon

Saber-toothed cats of the genus Smilodon *are known only from the Americas. There is evidence that at least the* S. fatalis *species lived and hunted in groups, much like lions.*

Three species of *Smilodon* are known. The earliest, *S. gracilis,* found mainly in the eastern United States, is the smallest. It is probably the species most closely related to *Megantereon, Smilodon*'s likely ancestor. The largest, *S. populator,* is found in the eastern part of South America and was of lion size, with enormously developed upper canines that protruded as much as 7 inches (18 cm) from the jaw. It had massive, relatively short, lower limb bones.

Social activity

The third species, *S. fatalis,* is intermediate in size and known mainly from the later Pleistocene of North America, although it also entered the western part of South America. It is the best-known species, thanks to the huge

Below: *A family of* Smilodon fatalis *sit in the shade of a tree. There is evidence of social activity among* Smilodon, *and maternal care is likely to have been important.*

Right: *The skeleton of* Smilodon populator *shows the massive development of this animal.*

126

Smilodon populator

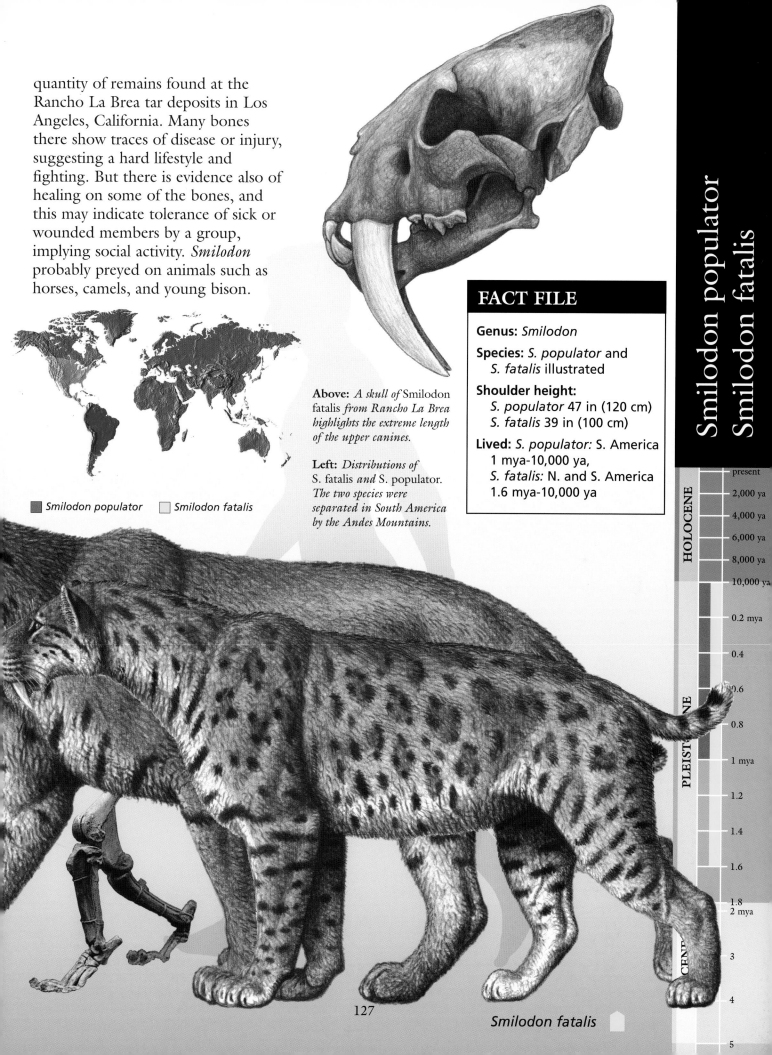

quantity of remains found at the Rancho La Brea tar deposits in Los Angeles, California. Many bones there show traces of disease or injury, suggesting a hard lifestyle and fighting. But there is evidence also of healing on some of the bones, and this may indicate tolerance of sick or wounded members by a group, implying social activity. *Smilodon* probably preyed on animals such as horses, camels, and young bison.

Smilodon populator   **Smilodon fatalis**

Above: *A skull of* Smilodon fatalis *from Rancho La Brea highlights the extreme length of the upper canines.*

Left: *Distributions of* S. fatalis *and* S. populator. *The two species were separated in South America by the Andes Mountains.*

FACT FILE

Genus: *Smilodon*

Species: *S. populator* and *S. fatalis* illustrated

Shoulder height:
S. populator 47 in (120 cm)
S. fatalis 39 in (100 cm)

Lived: *S. populator:* S. America 1 mya–10,000 ya,
S. fatalis: N. and S. America 1.6 mya–10,000 ya

present
2,000 ya
4,000 ya
6,000 ya
8,000 ya
10,000 ya
HOLOCENE

0.2 mya
0.4
0.6
0.8
1 mya
1.2
1.4
1.6
1.8
2 mya
PLEISTOCENE

3
4
5
CENE

127

Smilodon fatalis

Smilodon

A pair of Smilodon fatalis prowl the plains of late Pleistocene southwestern North America. Like big cats of today, the one on the right is roaring to proclaim his territory.

Hyenas

Prehistoric hyenas ranged in size and appearance from mongooselike animals up to "giant" species the size of a lion in the later development of the family.

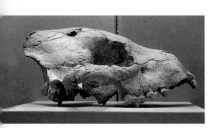

Above: *A skull of the catlike* Chasmaporthetes lunensis *shows teeth adapted for eating flesh rather than crunching bone.*

Below: *A scene depicting the hyena* Thalassictis *in pursuit of antelopes. Such hyenas were probably efficient pack-hunters, bringing down their prey by force of numbers.*

Hyenas belong to the family Hyaenidae. Only four of the 70 or so species of hyenas that have lived over the past 15 million years survive today. The largest is the spotted hyena, at weights up to 200 pounds (90 kg).

The earliest known hyenas were quite small animals, with a form suggesting an insectivorous or omnivorous lifestyle. They were similar to a mixture of living animals—smaller ones like mongooses and slightly larger ones like jackals and coyotes. The development of what we think of as the typical, larger animal equipped to scavenge and crush bones came late in the evolutionary history of the hyenas. It occurred about 5 million years ago with the appearance of a species known as *Adcrocuta eximia,* an animal about the size of a living spotted hyena.

But the most spectacular of the larger bone-crunchers was the giant, short-faced hyena (below), which originated

in Africa and spread into Eurasia. An animal with a huge head and large teeth, it stood nearly 39 inches (100 cm) high at the shoulders—almost as tall as a lion. These creatures must have been very efficient scavengers, able to drive off other predators from their kills, particularly if they acted in a large hunting group of the kind we see in living spotted hyenas.

Pachycrocuta brevirostris, the giant short-faced hyena, was larger than any of the living hyenas. It would have weighed perhaps 250 lb (113 kg) or more, making it comparable in size to a small lion. It first appeared in the later Pliocene of eastern and southern Africa, continuing there into the earlier Pleistocene. But it is better known from Eurasia, where it existed during the whole of the early Pleistocene.

Left: Pachycrocuta brevirostris *spread from Africa to Europe and Asia at least as far as China, where some of the best remains have been unearthed at the Zhoukoudian site.*

FACT FILE

Genus: *Pachycrocuta*

Species: *P. brevirostris* illustrated

Shoulder height: 39 in (100 cm)

Lived: Eurasia and Africa, 1.6-0.5 mya

Pachycrocuta brevirostris

HOLOCENE	present
	2,000 ya
	4,000 ya
	6,000 ya
	8,000 ya
	10,000 ya
PLEISTOCENE	0.2 mya
	0.4
	0.6
	0.8
	1 mya
	1.2
	1.4
	1.6
	1.8
	2 mya
PLIOCENE	3
	4
	5

Early ungulates

The first ungulates, or hoofed mammals, included both plant-eaters and meat-eaters. Among them, perhaps, was the largest known carnivorous land mammal—Andrewsarchus.

Phenacodus matthewi
Among some of the more advanced herbivorous condylarths were possible ancestors of the rhinos and horses. One such was *Phenacodus matthewi* from the early Eocene. This was a small animal, standing about 24 in (60 cm) at the shoulder, with long and unspecialized limbs ending in feet with five toes. It was probably a good runner, able to dodge predators in thick woodlands and to move well over difficult ground.

Hoofed mammals are today divided into two major groups, depending on their toes. The artiodactyls, or even-toed ungulates, have the major weight-bearing axis of the foot along the third and fourth toes. They are extremely diverse, with some 80 living genera. They include deer, sheep, goats, cattle, pigs, hippos, giraffes, and camels. Many, called ruminants, have a complex series of stomachs to allow a lengthy digestion process. Several long-extinct families are also included in this group. The perissodactyls, or odd-toed ungulates, once equally diverse, are represented today only by horses, rhinos, and tapirs. In this group, the axis of the foot passes through the third toe. In living horses, the toes are reduced to one.

Condylarths

Some of the most common mammals during the earliest Cenozoic era in Europe were primitive ungulates called condylarths. Although living ungulates are plant-eaters, the appearance of some condylarths suggests they were at least omnivorous, in the manner of a pig or, perhaps better still, a bear. There

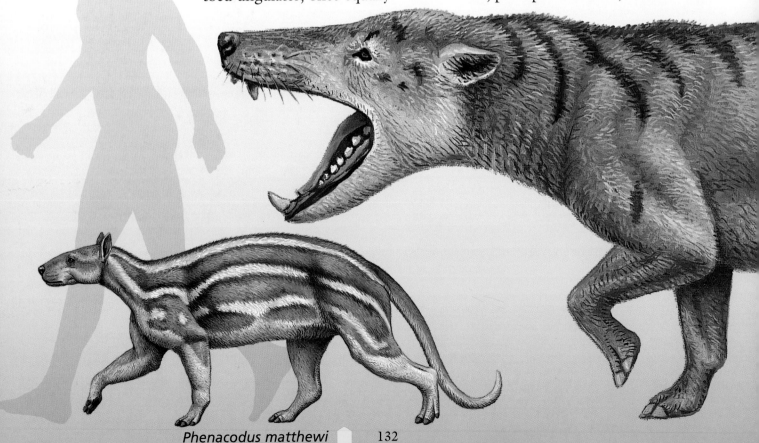

Phenacodus matthewi

Phenacodus   *Andrewsarchus*

Left: *The map shows distributions of* Andrewsarchus mongoliensis *and* Phenacodus matthewi.

Andrewsarchus mongoliensis Perhaps the most spectacular of the condylarths was *Andrewsarchus mongoliensis,* known from the later Eocene of Mongolia. With a skull 33 in (85 cm) long, it might have been the largest known land carnivore. No other bones have been found, but the skull was probably larger in proportion to its body than in living carnivores.

appear to have been no specialist carnivores of any great size among the rest of the mammals at this time. So a few species of condylarths might even have been active predators, perhaps like a hyena.

FACT FILE

Genus: *Phenacodus*

Species: *P. matthewi* illustrated

Shoulder height: 24 in (60 cm)

Lived: North America and western Europe, 55-52 mya

Genus: *Andrewsarchus*

Species: *A. mongoliensis* illustrated

Shoulder height: 4 ft 6 in (1.4 m)

Lived: Mongolia, 40 mya

Left: *A pair of* Phenacodus matthewi *moving cautiously through woodland in search of water—always a dangerous time for any herbivore because of a possible ambush.*

Andrewsarchus mongoliensis

MIOCENE	5 mya
	10
	15
	20 mya
OLIGOCENE	25
	30
	35
EOCENE	40 mya
	45
	50
	55
PALEOCENE	60 mya
	65

Dinocerates

Among the first of the large-bodied mammals were the dinocerates, animals the size of a large rhino with a brain the size of an apple. They are also known as uintatheres.

The dinocerates, or Uintatheriidae to give them their formal, family name, are a strange group of huge, superficially rhinolike animals. Their odd appearance, with large upper canines and a series of blunt hornlike structures on their heads, sets them apart from other mammals. Their relationship to other groups is unclear. They can be fairly described as being

among the first of the really large land mammals to appear in the fossil record. But their size was not reflected in their brains, which were remarkably small.

Opinions are divided as to whether Dinocerates originated in North America, where they are found in late Paleocene and Eocene deposits, or in Asia. But they certainly lived in both continents.

Below: *A skull of Uintatherium robustum clearly shows some of the bizarre features that distinguish the dinocerates. The series of bony "horns" contrasts with the long and pointed upper canine. And the massive appearance of the head contrasts with the rather slender lower jaw.*

Left: *Like other dinocerates,* Uintatherium *lived in North America.*

Uintatherium robustum, first found near Fort Bridger in Wyoming, is a typical species. The limbs must have been massive and rather elephant-like, but the skull is the outstanding feature. It has the usual series of bony lumps and protuberances, and the upper canine teeth are large—up to 12 inches (30 cm) in length—and downwardly pointing. The lower jaw looks relatively slender, and has a deep flange where the upper canine sits.

Numerous species are known, most bearing horns and elongated canines. The broad cheek teeth are not particularly high crowned, and point to a diet of leafy vegetation. The bizarre head structures suggest mating display. They may also indicate strong territorial defense.

Uintatherium robustum

135

MIOCENE	5 mya
	10
	15
	20 mya
OLIGOCENE	25
	30
	35
EOCENE	40 mya
	45
	50
	55
PALEOCENE	60 mya
	65

Primitive whales

Whales are descendants of four-legged land mammals, and are most closely related to hoofed animals. They gradually became more adapted to water some 50 million years ago.

Above: *A skull of* Pakicetus attocki *shows the many pointed teeth.*

Rodhocetus balochistanensis had ankle bones like those of primitive fossil artiodactyls. These creatures were adapted to life in water with feet that would not bear the weight of their bodies. At this stage, the commitment to life in water was almost complete. At best they might have struggled onto land like living seals or sea lions.

Living whales are placed in the order Cetacea, which includes dolphins and porpoises. Although they lack external rear limbs, their skeleton shows clearly that they descend from four-legged land mammals. The front flippers contain bones that match those in such land mammals. And some whales even retain a very reduced pelvis and rear limb, although these do not show outside the body. The precise relationship, however, has long been debated because of gaps in the fossil record. This is despite the fact that the substantial bones of whales fossilize extremely well. Recent studies of material from 52-million-year-old Eocene deposits in Pakistan now show that the earliest whales were not only land based, but were also efficient runners. Details of the ankle bones suggest that they are most closely related to artiodactyl ungulates—the even-toed hoofed group that includes antelope, hippos, and deer as well as giraffes and camels.

No modern equivalent

Some of the best Pakistani fossils belong to a species known as *Pakicetus attocki*. This is an animal about the size of a wolf, with a combination of whalelike features in its head and the body of an artiodactyl. There is no obvious modern equivalent of such an animal.

Rodhocetus balochistanensis

At about 45 million years ago, a further development occurred with the appearance of animals still more adapted to water. The best known is *Rodhocetus balochistanensis*, which had substantial hind legs that could have produced powerful swimming strokes. *Rodhocetus* lived in shallow seas, and might have had a similar lifestyle to seals or even dolphins. But it is not clear whether they ever came onto the land. Indeed, it is even likely that the feet would not have borne the weight of the animal. They might have been equipped with webbing between the toes to assist the swimming strokes.

Pakicetus attocki had a skeleton that was adapted to movement on land, much like many hoofed animals. They had an ear structure showing some adaptations for hearing under water, although not for the pressure of deep water. They also had a large and impressive set of teeth, indicating a predatory style of life. The picture built up is of a creature unlike anything alive today.

FACT FILE

Genus: *Rodhocetus*
Species: *R. balochistanensis* illustrated
Length: 9 ft 5 in (2.8 m)
Lived: Seas off southern Asia, 45 mya

Genus: *Pakicetus*
Species: *P. attocki* illustrated
Shoulder height: 24 in (61 cm)
Length: 6 ft 3 in (1.9 m)
Lived: Pakistan, 52 mya

Rodhocetus balochistanensis
Pakicetus attocki

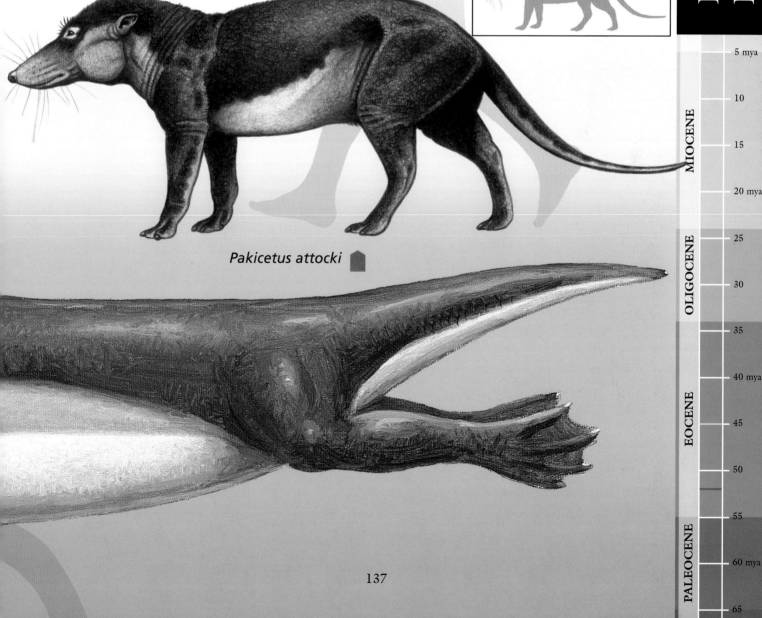

Pakicetus attocki

MIOCENE

OLIGOCENE

EOCENE

PALEOCENE

5 mya
10
15
20 mya
25
30
35
40 mya
45
50
55
60 mya
65

Whales

From living in water, whales have changed more than any other mammals, losing their hind limbs and using tail flukes for swimming. Their fossils reveal little of how these changes occurred.

Basilosaurus cetoides was a member of a group of large late Eocene whales that lived in most of the seas of the time. They showed a combination of whalelike features and characteristics that remind us of their land origins. For example, some members of the family retained well-grown hind limb bones, though the limbs did not show on the outside of the body. The name *Basilosaurus* means "king of the reptiles"—when the bones were first discovered, they were thought to belong to a dinosaur. But by the rules of animal nomenclature, a name once given correctly must stick, even if it turns out to be inappropriate!

The first whalelike animals we know of became fossilized about 50 million years ago in what is now Pakistan. With streamlined bodies and small, webbed hind flippers, they probably looked a bit like otters. Their teeth were suited for grasping and slicing slippery prey. Their ears were quite different from those of today's whales, and their hearing was like that of a modern sea lion. And it is certain they did not use echolocation. By the end of the Eocene, about 34 mya, whales lived in most of the world's seas. Some were dolphin-size and fed on fish. Others, such as *Basilosaurus*, grew much larger—up to 80 feet (25 m) long, though they had relatively small heads. They probably ate fish and other sea-living animals, for some of their teeth were capable of cutting flesh into pieces small enough to be swallowed. It is likely that they swam using horizontal tail flukes, for their bodies could be flexed like those of modern whales.

Toothed whales

Toothed whales evolved from such ancestors. One group, successful through much of the mid-Tertiary period, had saw-edged, triangular teeth, like those of some large sharks. Important changes involved the ear bones, so that we can trace the development of echolocation. Changes can also be traced in the shape of the face, making room for the fatty pad called the melon in living whales. At the same time, one of the nostrils, which were placed on the top of the head, became smaller, and today, all toothed whales have

only one external nostril, or blowhole. Such whales have changed little since the Miocene, when the seas contained dolphinlike creatures much like those of the present.

Baleen whales

The baleen, or plankton-feeding, whales descended from a toothed ancestor from the Antarctic that lived about 34 mya. The toothless forms evolved after the development of present-day patterns of ocean currents, which led to a great growth in plankton populations. These were able to sustain filter feeders such as the great whales. The shape of their toothless skulls suggests that they had plates of whalebone (baleen) hanging from the roof of the mouth, but these have not been preserved.

Eurhinodelphis bossi is one of a family of porpoiselike animals that lived in northern oceans in the Miocene period. Its long jaws were toothless at the tip, but behind this area was a series of small, pointed teeth, suitable for holding and manipulating slippery prey. At first sight it would have looked much like some of the Jurassic ichthyosaurs, marine reptiles that had the same kind of jaw structure.

FACT FILE

Genus: *Basilosaurus*

Species: *B. cetoides* illustrated

Length: 80 ft (25 m)

Lived: Worldwide, about 40-37 mya

Genus: *Eurhinodelphis*

Species: *E. bossi* illustrated

Length: 6 ft 6 in (2 m)

Lived: Worldwide, about 15 mya

Eurhinodelphis bossi

139

A scene set in the seas of the late Eocene with a pair of whales of the genus Basilosaurus. Compared with living large whales, their long and streamlined body contrasts oddly with their small head.

Enteledonts

Before large true mammalian carnivores evolved, the biggest meat-eaters around were the piglike enteledonts. These huge animals were probably more scavengers than hunters.

The enteledonts are members of the family Enteledontidae. Known from both North America and Europe from the late Eocene (about 35 mya) to the early Miocene (20 mya), they probably originated in Asia. They were distantly related to pigs. But although to the modern observer there is some family likeness, they were bizarrely, even monstrously, different. For one thing, they were large, with enormous heads up to 39 inches (1 m) in length. Their massive body was set on relatively long legs, and they had teeth more like those of a true carnivore.

Their strong forequarters and a short and robust neck supporting the huge head suggest they were powerful animals. They were reasonably well built for running, but the lower parts of their legs were short, so they were unlikely to have been fast. They probably scavenged, as their teeth would

Below: *A mounted skeleton of the North American enteledont* Archaeotherium, *at the County Museum of Los Angeles.*

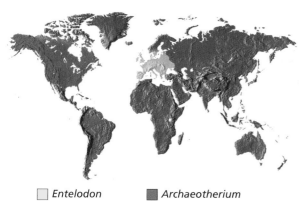

Left: Entelodon *were common in Europe during the Oligocene epoch. The similar North American genus* Archaeotherium *survived into the Miocene.*

☐ *Entelodon* ■ *Archaeotherium*

Entelodon deguilhemi was very similar to the American genus *Archaeotherium,* with bizarre knoblike structures on its lower jaw and cheekbones and an enormous head. The large tusklike canines show wear from biting, and the lower jaw could swing low, giving an enormous gape. These features, in combination with the size, shape, and wear on the other teeth, suggest a diet that included meat and perhaps bone.

have been effective bone-crushers. Whether any of them actually hunted is more difficult to determine. But they certainly outweighed any known specialist carnivore of the time. And they would have had little difficulty in seizing carcasses of animals brought down by more nimble predators.

FACT FILE

Genus: *Entelodon*

Species: *E. deguilhemi* illustrated

Shoulder height: 4 ft 5 in (1.3 m)

Lived: Europe, 34-32 mya

MIOCENE	5 mya
	10
	15
	20 mya
OLIGOCENE	25
	30
	35
EOCENE	40 mya
	45
	50
PALEOCENE	55
	60 mya
	65

Early Oligocene North America: The piglike Archaeotherium mortoni, standing only 43 inches (110 cm) at the shoulders, scares away a pair of Hesperocyon dogs from a water hole.

Hippopotamids

Hippos today live in the warm waters of Africa south of the Sahara. But fossil relatives have been found throughout Europe and as far north as Yorkshire, England.

Two species of hippopotamus live in Africa today. The small, forest-dwelling pygmy hippo of western Africa and the larger common hippo, *Hippopotamus amphibius,* are found mainly south of the Sahara. Common hippos are often seen in large herds—consisting chiefly of females—resting in water. They leave only at night to go in search of food—mainly tender grasses and other plants. Hippos may look peaceable, but ferocious fights sometimes take place as dominant males drive all possible rivals to the edge of the herd.

Earliest hippos

Fossil teeth and other fragments from rocks in Kenya, dating back about 20 million years, give us clues to the first hippos. The most common of them belonged to a genus called *Hexaprotodon.* These had a lighter skeleton and narrower feet than

Below: *A typical scene during the warmer periods of Europe in the mid-Pleistocene: A pair of hippos of the living species* Hippopotamus amphibius *share a water hole with animals such as early fallow deer and rhinos.*

Left: *The map shows the distribution of Hippopotamus gorgops in Africa.*

FACT FILE

Genus: *Hippopotamus*

Species: *H. gorgops* illustrated

Shoulder height: 5 ft (1.5 m)

Lived: Africa, 2.4-0.9 mya

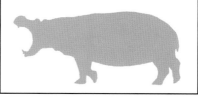

modern hippos, and their eyes did not protrude so much from the top of the face. This suggests that they spent far less time in water than modern common hippos do. During the Pleistocene period, some hippopotamuses moved north, eventually occupying much of Europe in the warm, interglacial phases of the Ice Age. The most northerly site known is at Victoria Cave, near Settle in Yorkshire, England, where they lived about 125,000 years ago.

Hippopotamus gorgops is closely related to living hippos. At least as big as a modern hippo, it was clearly at home in water, for its eyes were placed in raised sockets that look like turrets on the front of its skull. It was probably alert to all that was happening on the land when almost completely submerged. Strangely, in contrast to living hippos, its skeleton and feet are more like those of a pygmy hippo, suggesting it was equally at home on dry land.

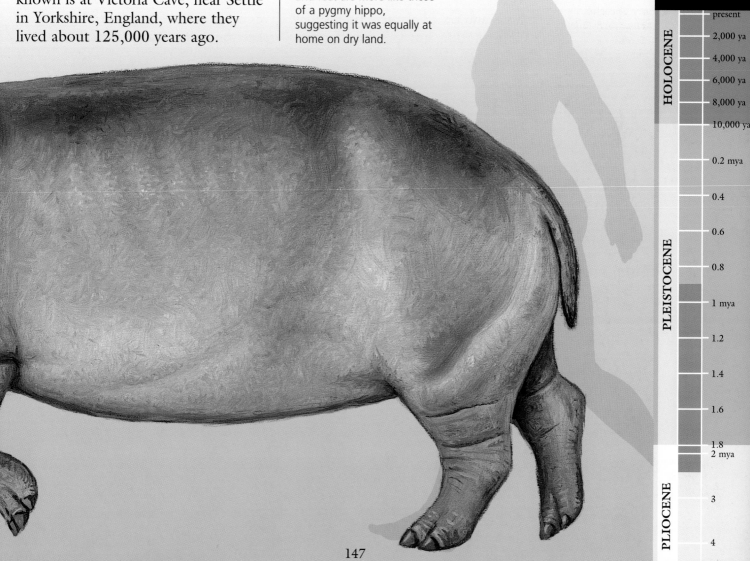

HOLOCENE	present
	2,000 ya
	4,000 ya
	6,000 ya
	8,000 ya
	10,000 ya
	0.2 mya
	0.4
	0.6
PLEISTOCENE	0.8
	1 mya
	1.2
	1.4
	1.6
	1.8 / 2 mya
PLIOCENE	3
	4
	5

Pigs

Fossil pigs were even more varied than living members of the family, the suids. They included some forms that reached the size of domestic cows—gigantic by modern standards.

Below: *A pair of listriodontine pigs of the mid-Miocene (15 mya) genus* Bunolistriodon. *These were medium-size animals that might have sought more leafy vegetation in their diet.*

The earliest fossil pigs are known from deposits in Eurasia some 30 million years ago. They first appeared in Africa—in Namibia and Kenya—about 17.5 mya. The family spread out extensively, with many subfamilies being created. Of these, the listriodonts were unusual in that the more evolved species had perhaps a greater amount of leafy vegetation in their diets, as opposed to the omnivorous fare of other suids. The males of the huge kubanochoerines had a kind of horn situated between the eyes. Another subfamily, the smaller hyotherids, might have been ancestors of the later pigs. The tetraconodontines replaced all of these subfamilies as the dominant group toward the end of the Miocene (10 mya). These were a group of pigs with thickened dental enamel, most typified by species of the genus *Nyanzachoerus* (below).

Piglet prey

The adult members of larger pig species would probably have been too

Nyanzachoerus syrticus Well-preserved skulls of this species from Miocene deposits at Lothagam, in Kenya, show that the males were large, with conspicuous ornamentation on the muzzle and widely flaring cheekbones. In life, these bony growths would have been augmented with an extra thickness of skin, making them even more spectacular. The tusks, however, were only of moderate size.

148   *Nyanzachoerus syrticus*

large and too aggressive for most of the predators. But the young of all pigs would have been an attractive prey, particularly before their tusks had begun to develop. And they are likely to have been left in a den while the adults foraged. Pigs have high reproduction rates in comparison with other ungulates. As a result, they might have provided a constant supply of piglets—a valuable source of food for any predator.

Kubanochoerus gigas were enormous pigs, with body weights of about 1,100 lb (500 kg) or more. Skulls found in Georgia and China show a well-developed frontal structure, rather like a horn. This might have been used in ritual fights between males, perhaps in the manner observed among African giant forest hogs today.

Below: *The first wild boars,* Sus scrofa, *appeared more than 1 mya in Europe. They eat a range of foods and are at home in woodlands.*

FACT FILE

Genus: *Nyanzachoerus*

Species: *N. syrticus* illustrated

Shoulder height: 39 in (1 m)

Lived: Eastern Africa, 7.5-2.5 mya

Genus: *Kubanochoerus*

Species: *K. gigas* illustrated

Shoulder height: 4 ft 1 in (1.2 m)

Lived: Georgia and China, 14 mya

Kubanochoerus gigas

149

PLEISTOCENE

10,000 ya
0.2 mya
0.4
0.6
0.8
1 mya
1.2
1.4
1.6
1.8
2 mya
3
4
5
10
15

MIOC

Camels and relatives

Camels have an origin very different from the sands of Arabia where most people now picture them. Their early development took place in North America, but they became extinct there 10,000 years ago.

Synthetoceras tricornatus, from the late Miocene of Texas, was a grazing species with high-crowned teeth. Like other members of the family, it had four toes on each foot, with those of the rear feet reduced to two functional toes. But the most marked features were the bony structures of the head. Whether these were covered with a horn, as in living cattle, is unclear, but they were certainly not shed each year like deer antlers.

Below: *A pair of* Paracamelus, *the first of the camelids to enter Eurasia, are depicted in late Miocene (5.8 mya) western Europe.*

Camels belong to the family Camelidae. We think of them now largely as animals of Arabia and the Sahara. But their fossil record runs from the Eocene of North America, and it is on that continent where most of the evolution of the family took place. Only in the late Miocene (5 mya) did they disperse into Eurasia and Africa. They became extinct in North America about 10,000 years ago.

Camels have an unusual pattern of movement termed "pacing," where both the front and the hind limb on one side move forward together. The earliest camels appear to have developed this pattern, as judged from footprint traces. They also seem to have developed elongated necks and shin bones reduced to a single, fused element. An extreme form of this development is seen in *Aepycamelus major* from North America (featured right). An animal with an almost giraffelike neck, it stood 10 feet (3 m) tall.

Unusual relatives

A second, now extinct North American family, the Protoceratidae, are thought to have been related to camels. They were somewhat different in overall appearance, although their lower limbs had similar structures that have led to their being grouped together. Some of the later members of this family developed

Synthetoceras tricornatus

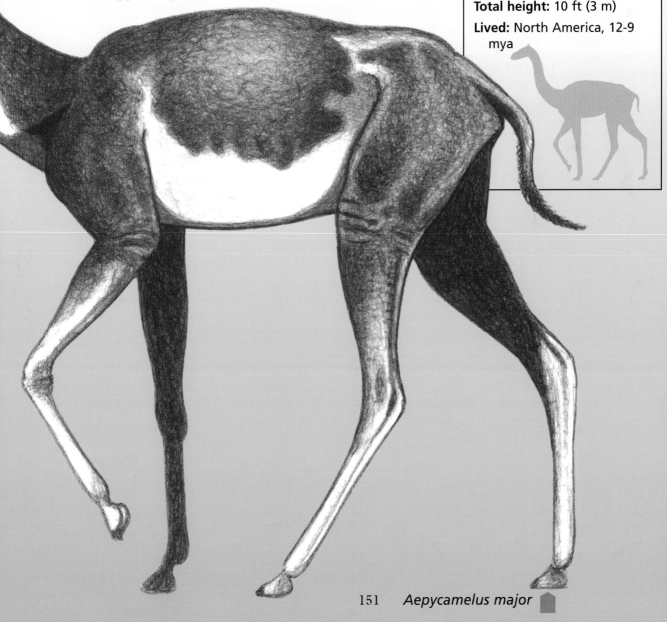

Left: *The map shows the distribution of the featured species in North America.*

□ *Synthetoceras*   ■ *Aepycamelus*

bizarre bony structures on a rather elongated head. These looked like a cross between cattle horns and deer antlers. One of the most extreme of these was *Synthetoceras tricornatus* from Texas (opposite page).

Aepycamelus major, with its long legs and very long neck, would have looked like a cross between a camel and a giraffe. Within the late Miocene wildlife of North America, it could be said to have had a giraffelike role, presumably feeding on high-level vegetation.

FACT FILE

Genus: *Synthetoceras*

Species: *S. tricornatus* illustrated

Shoulder height: 35 in (90 cm)

Lived: Texas, 12-9 mya

Genus: *Aepycamelus*

Species: *A. major* illustrated

Shoulder height: 7 ft 2 in (2.2 m)

Total height: 10 ft (3 m)

Lived: North America, 12-9 mya

Synthetoceras tricornatus
Aepycamelus major

5 mya	
MIOCENE	10
	15
	20 mya
OLIGOCENE	25
	30
	35
EOCENE	40 mya
	45
	50
	55
PALEOCENE	60 mya
	65

151   *Aepycamelus major* ▮

Deer and relatives

Thanks largely to their well-preserved antlers, deer have an excellent fossil record. Megaloceros giganteus was a giant among deer, with an antler span of up to nearly 12 feet.

Deer, members of the family Cervidae, or cervids, are a widely distributed group of hoofed animals. Unlike other ungulates with head ornaments—such as the giraffes with their ossicones and the bovids (cattle and relatives) with their horns—deer sport antlers. These are grown and shed annually and, except in the case of reindeer, are carried only by males. They are used to signal status, both to other males and to females. Because the antlers are often quite different from species to species and preserve well, deer have an excellent fossil record. They are known from at least 24 million years ago in Eurasia, where they have become a widespread feature of animal life over the past 5 million years. They also dispersed into North America and even into northern

Above: Arvernoceros ardei, *from the late Pliocene, was one of the first of the large European deer.*

Right: *On a flooded plain in late Pliocene Spain, a small group of deer* (Croizetoceros ramosus) *look around nervously as a family of mammoths pass by.*

Megaloceros giganteus was arguably the most impressive of the fossil deer. It flourished in Europe in the late Pleistocene, and is the largest known species, with a shoulder height of 6 ft 6 in (2 m) in males. The huge antlers had a spread of up to nearly 12 ft (3.5 m) and an estimated weight of around 110 lb (50 kg). Because this animal has been so commonly found in Irish bog deposits, it is often referred to as the Irish elk, although it was much more widely distributed than that—and it was not an elk.

Africa about 2 million years ago.

Most deer species are of moderate size, but toward the end of the Pliocene (1.8 mya) a series of larger-bodied species appeared, probably first in eastern Asia. Since antler size is related to body size, these larger species had impressive antlers, culminating in the truly enormous racks sported by the so-called Irish elk, *Megaloceros giganteus*.

FACT FILE

Genus: *Megaloceros*

Species: *M. giganteus*

Shoulder height: 6 ft 6 in (2 m)

Lived: Europe and western Asia, 500,000-10,000 ya

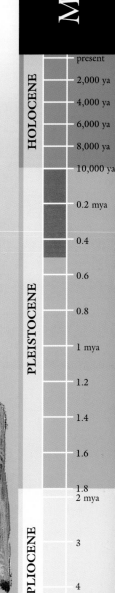

HOLOCENE	present
	2,000 ya
	4,000 ya
	6,000 ya
	8,000 ya
	10,000 ya
	0.2 mya
	0.4
	0.6
PLEISTOCENE	0.8
	1 mya
	1.2
	1.4
	1.6
	1.8
	2 mya
PLIOCENE	3
	4
	5

Megaloceros giganteus

Late Miocene: A couple of startled Cranioceras—three-horned deerlike mammals with hooves—flee a water hole in what is now Kansas, with a saber-toothed Nimravides in hot pursuit.

Deer

Antelope

Antelope, members of the largest and most diverse group of hoofed animals today, began to spread about 9 million years ago.

Above: *A skull of the antelope* Tragoportax gaudryi. *The horn cores of antelope provide good evidence for identification of species.*

Below: *Antelope of the species* Gazellospira torticornis *graze on a floodplain grassland in the Pliocene of Europe.*

The antelopes are members of the Bovidae, the family to which buffalo, domestic cattle, and even sheep and goats belong. The bovids are the most diverse of living ungulate families, with more than 70 species in Africa alone. They range in size from small gazelles to the large buffaloes and elands.

The most primitive of the living antelope is the nilgai, *Boselaphus tragocamelus.* This is a large and in some ways horselike animal found in high woodlands in India. It is placed in the bovid tribe Boselaphini, or boselaphines. Beginning in the middle Miocene of Eurasia, it was this group that began the process of bovid diversification into a large number of different genera.

The first known genus of the boselaphines in Europe is *Miotragocerus*, which is recorded in a number of localities from Georgia to Spain dating back to nearly 9 million years ago. *Miotragocerus pannoniae* is the best-known representative. It was a small to medium-size animal, weighing perhaps 175 pounds (80 kg). It had splayed hooves, suggesting a preference for wetter ground and a diet of relatively soft plants. Such animals would have been ideal prey for some of the larger saber-toothed cats of the period.

Miotragocerus pannoniae had body proportions and features similar to those of present-day antelope that live around water. This is particularly evident in the high rear and the widely splaying feet, which allowed it to move on wet ground. Water might also have offered an escape from predators, although tigers in India have learned to chase deer of around this size into water.

FACT FILE

Genus: *Miotragocerus*

Species: *M. pannoniae* illustrated

Shoulder height: 39 in (1 m)

Lived: Western Europe, 10–8 mya

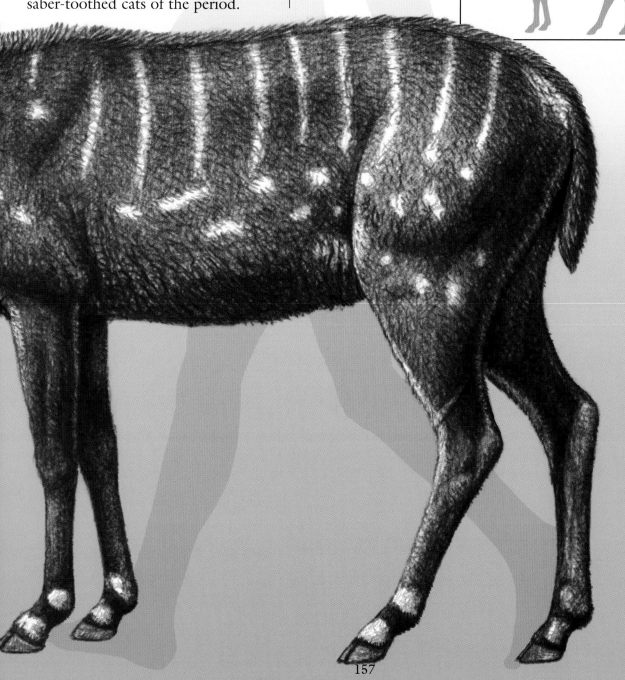

MIOCENE

OLIGOCENE

EOCENE

PALEOCENE

5 mya

10

15

20 mya

25

30

35

40 mya

45

50

55

60 mya

65

Cattle and bison

The horns of many living cattle and bison are large, but those of some of their fossil ancestors were enormous.

Bison priscus, also known as the steppe bison, was a Eurasian species that first appeared about 900,000 years ago. It seems to have dispersed to North America by 200,000 years ago. It was tall and powerfully built, with the long, upwardly swept horns and powerful shoulders of what we now think of as the typical bison. We may assume that it had the similar large herd structure where suitable grazing existed, and that it was a favorite prey of large predators, including humans.

Cattle, including our domestic breeds, as well as bison and buffalo belong to the same family as the antelopes, the Bovidae. Today, bison are found mainly in North America. There, enormous herds of the species *Bison bison*, what European settlers called buffalo, once provided food and other resources such as skins for many of the American Indians. The ancestors of American bison migrated from Eurasia during the Pleistocene. A small population of European bison, *Bison bonasus,* still exists in protected reserves. But during the ice ages, Europe was home to large numbers of these animals.

True buffaloes

The name "buffalo" comes from the Greek "boubalos," which meant an antelope or wild ox. Fossils of these true buffaloes are known from rocks of Pliocene age in Africa and Asia, where they spread widely in the Pleistocene. The water buffalo,

Bison priscus

158

Left: *The early Pleistocene bison of Europe, such as* Bison menneri *shown here in grasslands, were as tall as the later* B. priscus *species, but less robustly built and with smaller horns.*

Bubalus bubalis, now a native of Asia, even reached Europe during the warm interglacial phases. The heavy horned cape buffalo, which lives in much of Africa south of the Sahara, is the survivor of several Pleistocene species with enormous horns. *Pelorovis oldowayensis* was a giant among them. Its horn cores (the bony internal part of the horn) spanned 6 feet 6 inches (2 m), and each complete horn might have measured that length too. *P. antiquus* had horns that stretched sideways, like those of the Asiatic water buffalo. This huge animal died out only 10,000 years ago.

Pelorovis oldowayensis is best known from Olduvai Gorge, in Tanzania, where an associated skeleton and the remains of what might have been a herd were recovered. Although it was similar in size to a modern cape buffalo, the individual limb bones were considerably longer, making the animal taller. But the greatest differences were in the elongated skull and enormous horns, which project backward, then outward, and then forward. Such horns must have been for display rather than defense.

FACT FILE

Genus: *Bison*

Species: *B. priscus* illustrated

Shoulder height: 5 ft 9 in (1.8 m)

Lived: Eurasia, 900,000-10,000 ya; North America, 200,000-10,000 ya

Genus: *Pelorovis*

Species: *P. oldowayensis* illustrated

Shoulder height: 5 ft (1.5 m)

Lived: Africa, 1.8 mya-800,000 ya

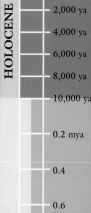

present
2,000 ya
4,000 ya
6,000 ya
8,000 ya
10,000 ya
0.2 mya
0.4
0.6
0.8
1 mya
1.2
1.4
1.6
1.8
2 mya
3
4
5

HOLOCENE
PLEISTOCENE
PLIOCENE

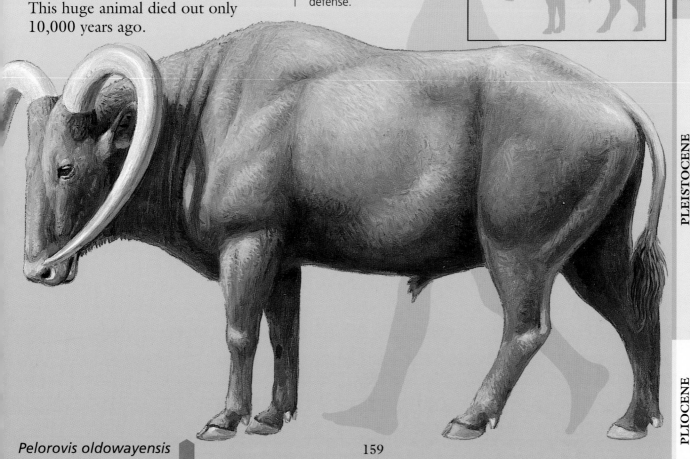

Pelorovis oldowayensis

Bison

A scene set 25,000 years ago during the last ice age in northern Spain, near the famous cave of Altamira. A group of steppe bison in the foreground are accompanied by a small herd of ibex seeking summer pasture.

Notoungulates

For much of the Cenozoic, South America was cut off from the rest of the world. Many of its mammals had no relatives elsewhere. The notoungulates were the largest order of ungulates, or hoofed mammals.

The large continent of South America had a unique combination of placental and marsupial mammals during its long isolation. The placental mammals included a large group of plant-eating ungulates. Many of these hoofed mammals must rank—to our eyes—as among the most bizarre animals known from the fossil record. Although precise interpretations vary, they are generally placed in four major orders. The largest of these are the notoungulates, with more than 100 genera ranging from rabbit size up to that of a hippopotamus or rhinoceros. They are followed in abundance by the litopterns, and smaller numbers of astrapotheres and pyrotheres, which are among the extraordinary animals found in Miocene rocks in Argentina.

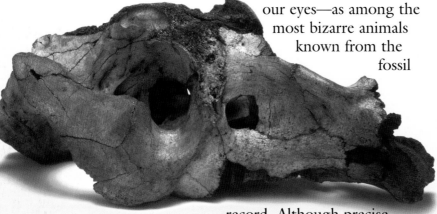

Above: *This skull of* Toxodon platensis, *now in the Natural History Museum in London, was found in Pleistocene deposits near Montevideo in Uruguay. Charles Darwin, who was taking a break from his voyage on the* Beagle *and traveling inland, heard of it and bought it—saving it from local boys who were making it a target for their stone throwing.*

Appearance

The appearance of all of these animals mimicked, to some extent, familiar creatures from other parts of the world. But this is doubtless a result of their environment—plains-dwelling runners tend to have long, slender limbs with a reduced number of toes, and grass-eaters have high-crowned teeth to deal with their tough food. Although we can reconstruct them in terms of today's deer, antelopes, horses, or rhinos, the details of their anatomy show them to be part of very different groups of animals.

Notoungulates

A very few, small notoungulates are known from early Eocene rocks in Wyoming and Mongolia, but these animals left no descendants. Perhaps they could not stand the competition outside South America,

Left: *Fossils of* Toxodon platensis *have been found in South America east of the Andes, from Bolivia to Patagonia.*

Toxodon platensis had the body bulk of a large rhino but with its hind limbs longer than the front. The large, shovel-like incisor teeth indicate a diet of water plants obtained through mud. The high-crowned teeth in the back of the jaw grew throughout the animal's life, compensating for wear caused by the grit mixed with its food. The nasal opening was high up on the face, suggesting it might have had a short trunk.

FACT FILE

Genus: *Toxodon*

Species: *T. platensis*

Shoulder height: 5 ft (1.5 m)

Lived: South America, 3 mya–10,000 ya (genus dates)

where they flourished. The South American notoungulates evolved into many forms, the last of them surviving through the Pleistocene. One of the best known of these animals was a hippo-size creature called *Toxodon platensis,* a specimen of which was collected by Charles Darwin during his famous voyage on the *Beagle.*

Toxodon

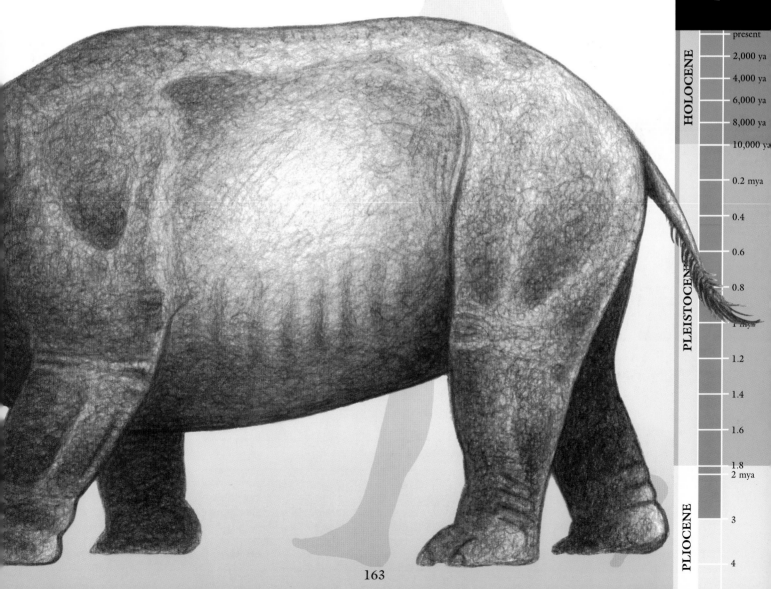

HOLOCENE	present
	2,000 ya
	4,000 ya
	6,000 ya
	8,000 ya
	10,000 ya
	0.2 mya
	0.4
	0.6
	0.8
PLEISTOCENE	1 mya
	1.2
	1.4
	1.6
	1.8
	2 mya
PLIOCENE	3
	4
	5

Litopterns

This extinct order of ungulates includes gazellelike animals as well as some heavyweights the size of camels. They are alike in their low-crowned teeth and the form of their ankle joint.

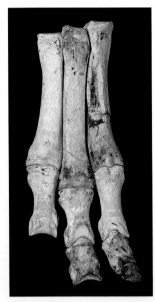

After the notoungulates, the litopterns are the second largest order of South American hoofed mammals. The group gets it name from its ankle joint—litoptern means "simple ankle." Some litopterns, including the biggest known, *Macrauchenia patachonica,* survived into the Pleistocene epoch. A large animal with a body length of about 10 feet (3 m), it had a long neck and a short, elephant-like trunk. These features must have given it access to the lower branches of trees on which it browsed for food.

Other litopterns, such as the slightly smaller *Diadiaphorus,* were much more horselike. The similarity extended to long legs and the reduction of the foot to give a single weight-bearing toe. But their teeth were not as specialized for grazing. One group of litopterns developed into pony-size creatures that must have looked much like short-necked horses.

Like horses, they ran from their enemies on long, single-toed legs, escaping not from carnivorous mammals, but from huge, flightless,

Above: *These foot bones of* Macrauchenia patachonica *were collected in Argentina early in 1834 by the British naturalist Charles Darwin during a break taken from his ship the* Beagle.

Below: *A puma is shown attacking* Macrauchenia *feeding in Bolivian woodland during the late Pleistocene. The young of ungulates would have been a prime target for such a predator.*

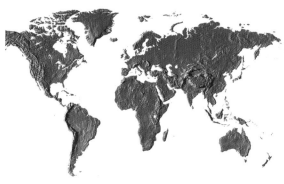

Left: *Fossils of* Macrauchenia patachonica *have been found from Bolivia to Patagonia.*

flesh-eating birds that lived on the Miocene plains of Patagonia, in southern Argentina.

But the presence of intelligent carnivores such as pumas and jaguars, which had streamed into South America once a land bridge with the North had been established, spelled the end for all of these native hoofed animals.

Macrauchenia patachonica must have looked like a humpless, thick-legged camel, although the three toes on its feet were more like those of a rhino. Its strangest feature was the head. Perched on a long neck, the skull was only 18 in (45 cm) long. The nasal opening was nearly on top of the head, suggesting that it had a short, but elephant-like trunk, which probably helped it to grasp its food.

FACT FILE

Genus: *Macrauchenia*

Species: *M. patachonica*

Shoulder height: 5 ft (1.5 m)

Lived: South America, 700,000-10,000 ya

Macrauchenia patachonica

	present
HOLOCENE	2,000 ya
	4,000 ya
	6,000 ya
	8,000 ya
	10,000 ya
	0.2 mya
	0.4
	0.6
PLEISTOCENE	0.8
	1 mya
	1.2
	1.4
	1.6
	1.8
	2 mya
PLIOCENE	3
	4
	5

Litopterns

South America in the Pleistocene: Three *Macrauchenia patachonica* flee from a pair of Smilodon populator.
These saber-tooths were probably the only predators capable of taking adults of these strange animals.

Astrapotheres

Astrapotheres were among several groups of hoofed animals that flourished in the early part of the Cenozoic era but became extinct before the end of the Miocene epoch.

The first astrapotheres developed in South America soon after the last of the dinosaurs had disappeared. They were small creatures, but their descendants were larger. Before the end of the Eocene some were as big as modern tapirs. And during the Oligocene some grew to be bigger than rhinos.

In many ways astrapotheres are a puzzle. They had long, heavy bodies. But, unlike almost all other mammals, their forelimbs, though short, were much more heavily built than their back legs. They had small, plantigrade (flat-footed) feet, which might have suited them for life in a swampy habitat.

The shape of the skull or teeth often gives good clues to an animal's lifestyle, but not in the astrapotheres. We can see that the front of the skull is very short with no upper incisors, though the canine teeth are very large and grew throughout the animal's life. The spadelike lower incisors were probably used for cutting vegetation that was then chewed up by the high-crowned teeth in the back of the mouth.

Below: *This complete skeleton of* Astrapotherium magnum *is in the Field Museum of Natural History, Chicago. From it, the apparently conflicting features of large size with feeble legs, and a trunk on a head and neck that can reach the ground, can easily be seen.*

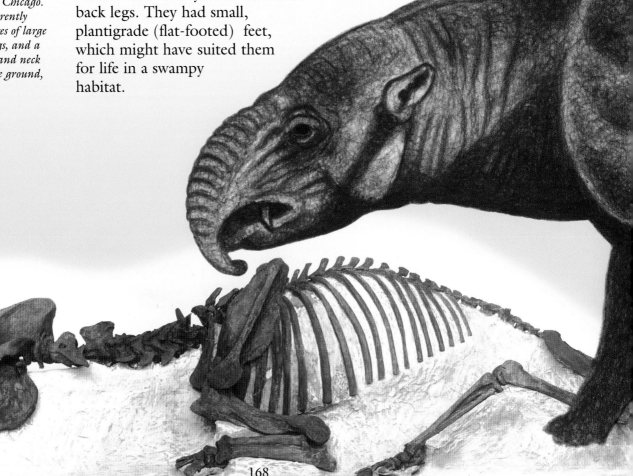

Left: *Fossil remains of Astrapotherium magnum have been found in the Santa Cruz volcanic ash beds in southern Argentina.*

Astrapotherium magnum has puzzled many scientists who have tried to discover how it lived. The feeble legs and heavy body suggest that it might have spent its time partly supported by water. The high-crowned teeth tell us that it fed on harsh food, yet most floating water plants have soft tissues. Perhaps it used its trunk to wrench hard rushes from the shallows while it remained safe in deeper water.

FACT FILE

Genus: *Astrapotherium*

Species: *A. magnum* illustrated

Shoulder height: 45 in (114 cm)

Lived: Argentina, 18-15 mya

The top of the head was domed, but the brain case was small. The nasal opening was high up on the head, so this strange creature apparently had a short trunk, which might have been used for grasping food.

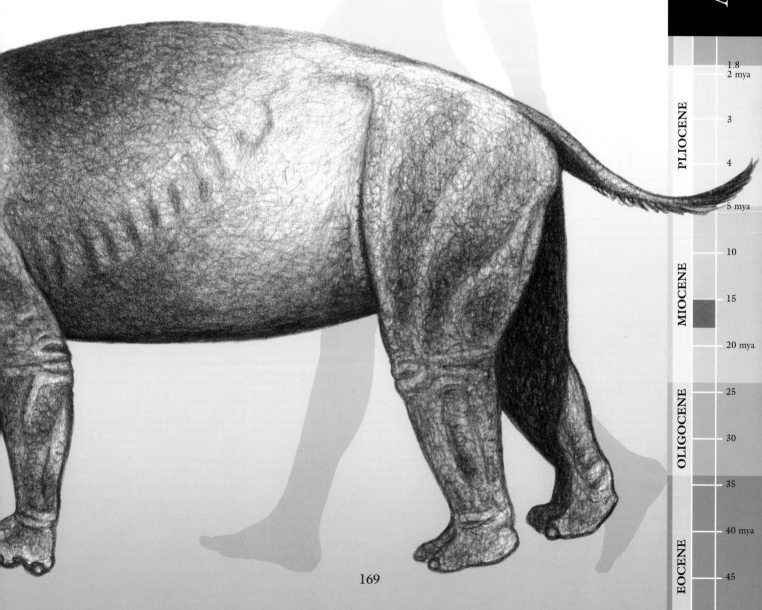

PLIOCENE

1.8
2 mya

3

4

5 mya

MIOCENE

10

15

20 mya

OLIGOCENE

25

30

35

EOCENE

40 mya

45

Palaeotheres

Perissodactyls, hoofed mammals with an odd number of toes, carry their weight on the middle toe of each foot. Among them are the now extinct palaeotheres, once thought to be early horses.

Propalaeotherium hassiacum lived in forests near what is now Messel in Germany. Its fossil shows it as a small, stocky animal, with a fairly short neck and short front legs—suggesting it was not a very speedy creature. Though the actual color was lost, there are indications that its coat was blotched with different shades. This would have camouflaged it in habitats where predators could approach unseen.

Below: *A complete skeleton of* Palaeotherium magnum. *This specimen is so completely preserved that a study of its stomach contents was possible. It had been eating leaves and grapelike fruit.*

Early in the Eocene epoch, about 50 million years ago, a great many different kinds of browsing plant-eaters evolved. Today, the only survivors from the ancient hosts of the so-called "odd-toed" hoofed mammals are the horses, rhinos, and tapirs. And of these, apart from domestic horses and the plains zebra in Africa, all are endangered species.

The first palaeotheres were forest-dwelling browsers, rather like tapirs with short, stout legs. Most were fairly small, although some grew to the size of ponies, and one, at least, was as big as a rhino. Some of them had teeth that looked very much like those of horses. As a result, there has been much confusion between early horse ancestors and palaeotheres. A fossil, thought at first to be like a hyrax and named *Hyracotherium leporinum*, was later regarded as the first horse *(Eohippus)*. Only more recently was it suggested that it might belong to a separate family, the palaeotheres.

Occasionally, conditions are right for the perfect preservation of fossils. This happened about 49 million years ago at Messel in Germany. There, fine sediment covered many animals soon after they died. One such species was the palaeothere *Propalaeotherium hassiacum*, which shows great details

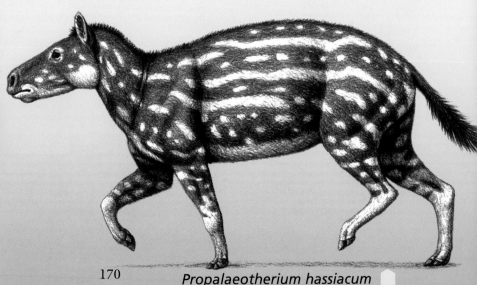

Propalaeotherium hassiacum

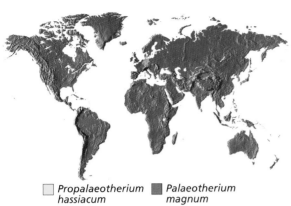

☐ *Propalaeotherium hassiacum* ■ *Palaeotherium magnum*

Left: *Both* Propalaeotherium hassiacum *and* Palaeotherium magnum *lived in Europe during the Eocene epoch.*

Palaeotherium magnum is well known from an almost complete skeleton found at Mormoiron, in France. This shows that it had a horselike head set on an elongated neck, and relatively long front legs. But the limbs were fairly heavy, indicating it was a rather slow-moving browser. It would have been capable of taking leaves from trees and shrubs up to about 6 ft (2 m) from the ground.

of its structure and even the contents of its stomach. A skeleton of another palaeothere, *Palaeotherium magnum*, is also preserved in great detail from a site in France.

FACT FILE

Genus: *Propalaeotherium*

Species: *P. hassiacum* illustrated

Shoulder height: 20 in (52 cm)

Lived: Germany, 49 mya

Genus: *Palaeotherium*

Species: *P. magnum* illustrated

Shoulder height: 4 ft 8 in (1.4 m)

Lived: France, 36 mya

Palaeotherium magnum

171

Propalaeotherium hassiacum
Palaeotherium magnum

	5 mya
MIOCENE	10
	15
	20 mya
OLIGOCENE	25
	30
	35
	40 mya
EOCENE	45
	50
	55
PALEOCENE	60 mya
	65

Rhinoceroses

Today's five species of rhinoceroses are a tiny remnant of the huge number of rhinos that lived in the past. Some were lightweight runners, others gigantic, heavy, and probably slow-moving.

Rhinoceroses lived on the northern continents during the last 40 million years. Most had heavy skeletons, which tend to be well preserved. But besides this, we have evidence of rhinos preserved in the permafrost in the far north. Also, from a site in eastern Europe, a woolly rhino, *Coelodonta antiquitatis* (together with a mammoth and three other rhinos), was found pickled in a mixture of oil and brine that saturated the swampy area where it lived. Our own ancestors knew some now extinct rhinos as living animals, and occasionally painted them on cave walls in France and Spain.

Below: Stephanorhinus hemitoechus, *sometimes called the narrow-nosed rhino, lived during the later interglacial periods in Europe. It was a large animal, but slender and long-legged compared with the cold-climate woolly rhino.*

Sea levels were very low during the time of woolly rhinos, and there was a land bridge between Asia and America across the Bering Strait. Woolly mammoths made this crossing, but, strangely, the rhinos did not.

The heavyweights

Of the many rhinos that lived in the Oligocene epoch (34-24 mya), some were tapirlike with teeth that indicate they were mainly browsers. Much more spectacular were the heavyweights, which include the biggest of all known land mammals, the indricotheres

(see pages 174-5). In the Miocene (from 24 mya), rhinos related to present forms made their appearance. Some had horns, some had heavy coats. The limbs of some suggest they lived rather like modern hippos. One rhino, *Teleoceras,* which was the same size as living rhinos, had a brain that was twice as big.

Left: *A small group of the hornless rhino* Hispanotherium, *known from mid-Miocene times in Turkey and Spain. These long-legged rhinos were specialist grazers with high-crowned teeth.*

Coelodonta antiquitatis, the woolly rhino, is known from countless finds from the last part of the ice age. Its long coat and compact body shape helped it survive in the cold conditions. Rhino horns are made of compressed hair and rarely survive, but some woolly rhino horns have been preserved in frozen permafrost specimens. Wear on the lower surface suggests these might have been used to sweep snow away from their food. This would have consisted mainly of the tough grasses of the steppes (grasslands) of Asia, its chief habitat.

FACT FILE

Genus: *Coelodonta*

Species: *C. antiquitatis*

Shoulder height: 5 ft 6 in (1.7 m)

Lived: Eurasia, 200,000-10,000 ya

present
2,000 ya
4,000 ya
6,000 ya
8,000 ya
HOLOCENE
10,000 ya
0.2 mya
0.4
0.6
0.8
1 mya
1.2
1.4
1.6
1.8
2 mya
PLEISTOCENE
3
4
5

Indricotheres

The largest known land mammals were giant rhinos that stood 20 feet (6 m) at the shoulder and weighed at least twice as much as a bull African elephant.

Below: *A group of* Indricotherium *browse untroubled by the presence of two creodonts of the wolf-size species* Hyaenodon dubius. *Even a newborn calf would have been too big for such small predators to tackle.*

Among the great number of rhino species, some, called the indricotheres, grew to gigantic size—exceeded among mammals only by some of the larger whales. Their fossils have been found in Oligocene rocks in parts of central Asia, from China in the east to as far west as the republic of Georgia. Their strong, pillarlike limbs held up a heavy body, a stout neck several feet long, and a big head. The teeth were suited to chewing moderately tough leaves and twigs. And the body would have housed a gut that could process huge amounts of food. Like many rhinos of the past, these giants were hornless. The males

might have had other methods of showing their dominance, and such huge animals hardly needed horns for defense. Even newborns would have been very large. With the protection of their mothers, they would have been too much for the predators of the time to tackle.

Extinction

Although great size can be a help in survival, it carries some downsides. Perhaps because of these, the Indricotheres did not survive much beyond the end of the Oligocene. One disadvantage is the amount of food needed to fuel such giant bodies. If conditions change and food plants become scarce, the population

Left: *In Oligocene times,* Indricotherium transouralicum *ranged from China and Mongolia to Georgia.*

Indricotherium transouralicum (the genus is sometimes called *Paraceratherium* or *Baluchitherium*). No complete skeleton of this animal has ever been found. But enough bones are known for scientists to be able to estimate that it stood about 20 ft (6 m) at the shoulder. With its long neck, it could browse on leaves growing more than 25 ft (8 m) above the ground. Its weight would have been at least 15 tons. So it and its very close relatives are, by a long way, the tallest and the heaviest of all land mammals, past and present.

FACT FILE

Genus: *Indricotherium*
Species: *I. transouralicum*
Shoulder height: 20 ft (6 m)
Lived: Eurasia, 29-23 mya

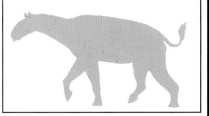

may drop. And since large animals generally produce only a single young one, often at intervals of at least two years, it would be difficult to rebuild their numbers quickly. Another difficulty inherent in large size is the tendency to overheat. Such giants as the indricotheres could have been in real trouble if they had to travel long distances in search of food.

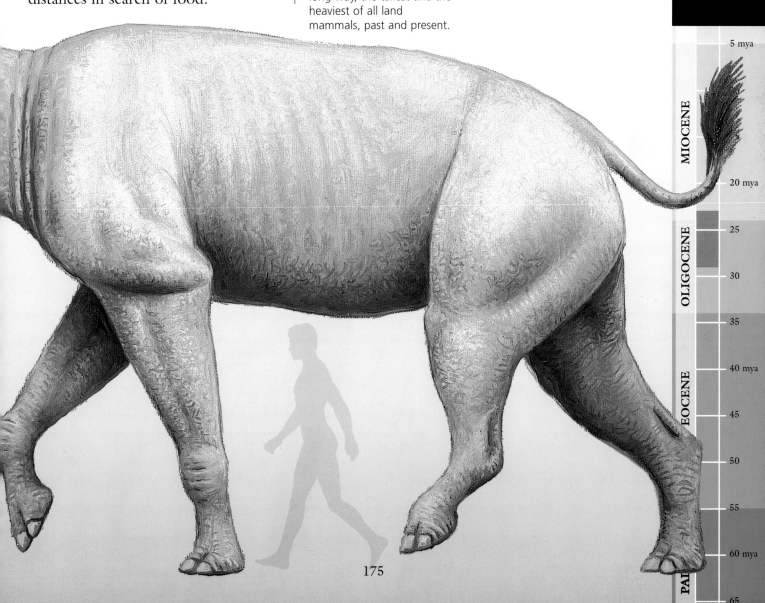

Indricotherium transouralicum

5 mya

MIOCENE

20 mya

25

OLIGOCENE

30

35

40 mya

EOCENE

45

50

55

60 mya

PA

65

Chalicotheres

The Chalicotheres are an extinct group of plant-eaters with long, clawed front limbs that helped them to browse from the branches of trees.

Chalicotherium grande lived in Europe in the Miocene period. It had a strong pelvis and hind legs, which enabled it to sit, and possibly even to stand, on its hind legs to reach up to branches unavailable to smaller browsers. Although the last relatives of these animals are thought to have become extinct in the Pleistocene, people traveling in the forests of Kenya have sometimes brought back tales of a strange animal with long, clawed forelimbs and a horselike face. Perhaps a descendant of the chalicotheres still survives.

Below: Phyllotillon *from the early Miocene of Europe looked somewhat like a heavyset horse.*

The name "chalicothere" was given to these distant relatives of the horses and rhinos because the shape of their grinding teeth, when worn, looks like a chalice, or goblet. Although they seem never to have been common, fossils have been found in rocks of various ages through the Cenozoic era. Chalicotheres lived in North America, Asia, Europe, and Africa, where they finally became extinct in the time of the ice age.

They were plant-eaters and had horselike faces. But they had heavier bodies than horses, and their front legs were much longer than their hind legs. Like rhinos, chalicotheres had three toes on each foot. Those on the front feet had huge, in-turned claws, so long that the animals walked on turned-over knuckles.

The uses of claws

Almost certainly chalicotheres used their clawed front limbs to pull down branches of trees, so they could browse the succulent foliage. It is also possible that they might have dug for roots and tubers, but their teeth do not show the

Chalicotherium grande

Left: *Distributions of* Tylocephalonyx skinneri *in North America and* Chalicotherium grande *in Europe.*

☐ *Tylocephalonyx skinneri*   ■ *Chalicotherium grande*

FACT FILE

Genus: *Chalicotherium*
Species: *C. grande* illustrated
Shoulder height: 6 ft (1.8 m)
Lived: Europe, 10-8 mya

Genus: *Tylocephalonyx*
Species: *T. skinneri* illustrated
Shoulder height: 5 ft (1.5 m)
Lived: North America, 19-15 mya

sort of wear that such gritty food would cause.

Members of a related group, the schizotheriines, which included *Tylocephalonyx skinneri* (below), were more horselike in their general proportions. But they had claws on all four feet. They must have competed successfully with other herbivores, because they did not become extinct until about 2 million years ago.

Tylocephalonyx skinneri from the Miocene of North America had many of the chalicothere features that seem so odd to modern eyes—elongated front legs, clawed hooves, and a long neck ending in a broadly horselike head. But in addition, it had an even stranger feature in the shape of a domed skull. This might have served as a reinforced region for head-butting contests between males competing for mates.

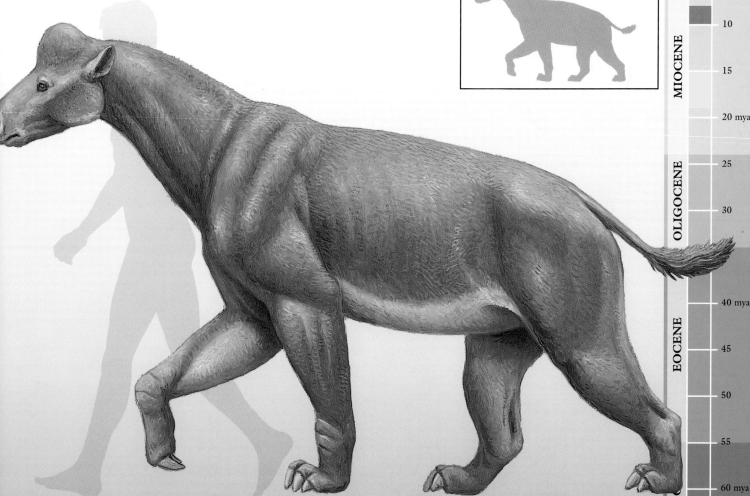

Tylocephalonyx skinneri

177

5 mya
10
15
20 mya
MIOCENE
25
30
OLIGOCENE
40 mya
45
EOCENE
50
55
60 mya
PALE
65

Early horses

The first horses that can be identified from fossil remains were small creatures. They had a flexible, doglike back, unlike the straight back of today's horses.

Orohippus agilis is one of the first members of the horse family, known from 52-million-year-old deposits in Wyoming and Oregon. It was a small, forest-dwelling creature, standing only about 16 in (40 cm) at the shoulder. It had fairly short legs and a stocky, rather curved body. Its eyes looked forward, and it developed long jaws to accommodate bigger teeth developing in the back of its mouth. As a result, its head had something of the look of a horse about it.

Early horses reached North America from Europe and Asia when all these northern continents formed a continuous landmass. Horse evolution progressed in North America, and the main changes in horselike animals occurred there. There were many kinds of horses. Some lived in the forests. Others took to life on the open plains. Later species tended to be large, though none developed into real giants. Today's horses are all long-legged, single-toed grass-eaters—the only branch of a complex family tree to have survived.

True horses

Some of the earliest known horses

come from fossil finds in Oregon and Wyoming. They lived about 52 million years ago, and have been given the name *Orohippus*. They were small, browsing creatures, with teeth suited to eating soft leaves from trees and shrubs. But they heralded the changes that would make their descendants into true horses. The most important of these was an increase in size of the premolar teeth, providing a greater grinding area. As their descendants moved onto the plains, other changes occurred. The eyes moved

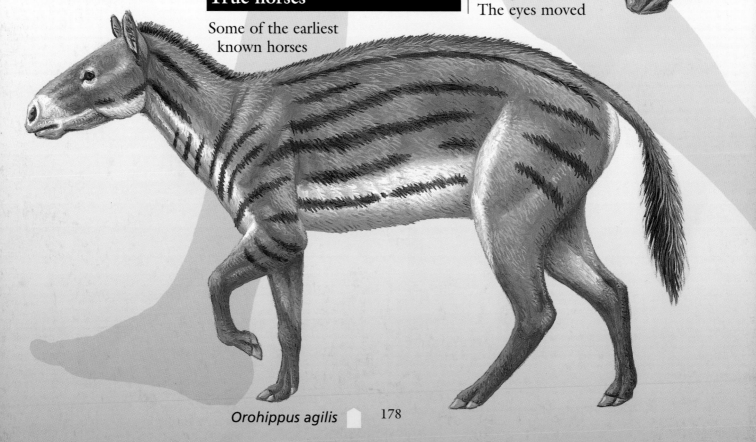

Orohippus agilis 178

FACT FILE

Genus: *Orohippus*

Species: *O. agilis* illustrated

Shoulder height: 16 in (40 cm)

Lived: Western North America, 52-45 mya

Genus: *Mesohippus*

Species: *M. bairdi* illustrated

Shoulder height: 21 in (54 cm)

Lived: North America, 37-32 mya

back up the face and outward, enabling later horses to spot predators creeping up on them from behind.

Oligocene horses

By Oligocene times many kinds of horses had developed in North America. They were bigger than the early species and all had only three toes on both front and back feet. The premolar teeth had grown to equal the molars in size, increasing the efficiency of the jaws.

Mesohippus bairdi is found in Oligocene deposits in Colorado and Canada. It stood about 21 in (54 cm) at the shoulder and had slender, longer legs and a more horselike body than its predecessors. Like the hind feet, the forefeet had only three toes. So though *Mesohippus* was a forest-dweller, it was better able to run from its enemies than earlier horses had been, for each foot weighed less and could be carried forward more easily.

Mesohippus bairdi   179

Orohippus agilis
Mesohippus bairdi

5 mya

MIOCENE

10

15

20 mya

OLIGOCENE

25

30

35

40 mya

EOCENE

45

50

55

PALEOCENE

60 mya

65

Later horses

Horses continued to evolve in North America. Some spread back into Asia and Europe, where they survived, but those left in America eventually died out.

Above: *A group of* Equus stenonis, *from the late Pliocene of Europe. The teeth and proportions of this species are more like those of zebras than true horses.*

Right: *An incomplete skull of* Anchitherium.

The evolution of horses was complex. But the overall trend was toward a bigger, faster-running, grazing plains animal. By the Oligocene epoch, all horses had three toes on each foot. Though heavier than the single-toed foot of modern horses, three toes gave stability. However, the outer toes tended to become smaller—by the end of the Miocene, they rarely if ever supported the creature's weight. With this came

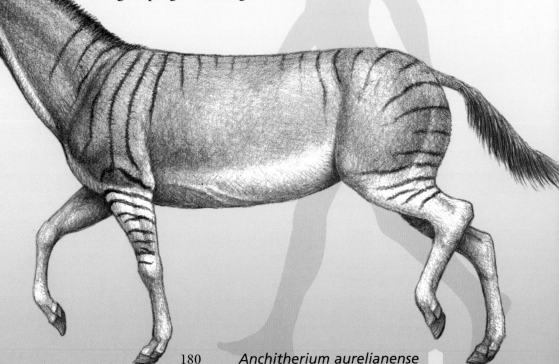

a fusing and strengthening of some of the leg bones, so that galloping over rough ground became possible. Other modern features included teeth designed for chewing abrasive grasses rather than leaves.

As new species evolved in America, they spread over the continent, some getting as far as the land bridge that existed between Alaska and Asia. Once across, they traveled through the forests and steppes into Europe. The first to do this, in the Oligocene, were three-toed horses called anchitherines. Then, in the mid-Miocene, hipparionine horses (genus *Hipparion* and their relatives), reached the Old World, where they survived until the early Pleistocene. By this time true single-toed horses of the modern genus *Equus* had arrived from America, to take over as

Anchitherium aurelianense was an anchitherine, one of the three-toed horses that reached Eurasia during the Oligocene. Though small, it was much more horselike in general appearance than any of the Eocene species had been. Its body, neck, and legs were all fairly long, but its face was shorter than in living horses. This was probably because the jaws contained low-crowned teeth, smaller than those of grazing horses but well suited to its diet of leaves.

Anchitherium aurelianense

Left: A pair of male asslike horses, Equus altidens, from the early Pleistocene of Europe fight to gain access to the females of the herd.

Below left: In this Hipparion *skull, the opening to the right of center is the eye socket. The cavity left of center is called the preorbital opening. Its purpose is unknown, and it is not present in modern horses. But its position is used in the classification of fossil horses.*

Hippotherium primigenium was a *Hipparion*-like horse of the late Miocene. Standing nearly 5 ft (1.5 m) at the shoulders, it was much larger than earlier horses. It still had three toes on each foot, although one toe took nearly all of its weight. Its teeth were large, so it might have been partly a browser. But it was probably at home in open country as well as woodlands.

supremely efficient grazing animals. Strangely, the horses left in America eventually died out, and there were no horses on the continent until they were reintroduced by the Spaniards in the 1500s.

FACT FILE

Genus: *Anchitherium*

Species: *A. aurelianense* illustrated

Shoulder height: 41 in (105 cm)

Lived: Eurasia, 26 mya

Genus: *Hippotherium*

Species: *H. primigenium* illustrated

Shoulder height: 5 ft (1.5 m)

Lived: Europe, 9 mya

5 mya
10
MIOCENE
15
20 mya
25
OLIGOCENE
30
35
40 mya
EOCENE
45
50
55
PALEOCENE
60 mya
65

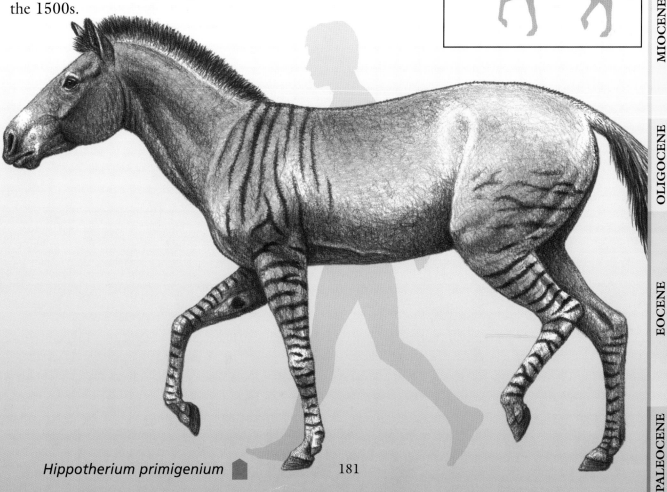

Hippotherium primigenium

Later horses

The floodplains of late Miocene Greece, with their grassy, open woodlands and standing water, offered an excellent habitat for these hipparionine horses. Grazing provided an important part of their diet

Brontotheres

The brontotheres started out the size of dogs, but evolved into rhino-size animals with bizarre horn structures. Because of their size, the group is also known as the titanotheres.

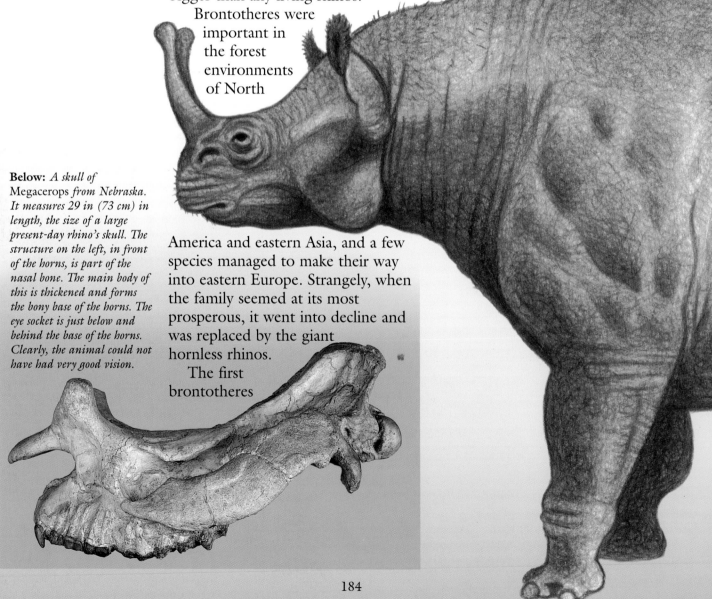

In the Eocene, members of the brontotheres were only about the size of a collie dog. Yet they evolved into some of the most spectacular of fossil mammals. In the Oligocene, when the group was at its most diverse, it included horned giants bigger than any living rhinos.

Brontotheres were important in the forest environments of North America and eastern Asia, and a few species managed to make their way into eastern Europe. Strangely, when the family seemed at its most prosperous, it went into decline and was replaced by the giant hornless rhinos.

The first brontotheres were similar to the earliest horses. But they diverged, increasing in size and often developing a horn on the end of the snout. This horn was sometimes forked, and the structure of the nasal bone suggests it was

Below: *A skull of* Megacerops *from Nebraska. It measures 29 in (73 cm) in length, the size of a large present-day rhino's skull. The structure on the left, in front of the horns, is part of the nasal bone. The main body of this is thickened and forms the bony base of the horns. The eye socket is just below and behind the base of the horns. Clearly, the animal could not have had very good vision.*

Left: *A distribution map of* Megacerops coloradensis *in North America.*

covered with skin, like the ossicones of the present-day giraffe.

Throughout their history, brontotheres had teeth suited for chewing nothing more than tender leaves. Even the teeth of the very big species were no more than inefficient "millstones." In times of food shortage, this could be a disaster, and might have been largely responsible for their extinction.

Megacerops coloradensis, formerly called *Brontotherium,* had a bulky body the size of a large rhino, though its head seemed small, perched on the heavy neck. The strangest and most obvious feature was the large, forked horn on the end of its face. The horns of the males were bigger than those of the females, so it is likely they were used for display—in the competition for food, territory, or mates. They were probably not used in defense against predators, as sheer size can be protection enough.

FACT FILE

Genus: *Megacerops*

Species: *M. coloradensis* illustrated

Shoulder height: Up to 8 ft (2.5 m)

Lived: North America, 37-33 mya

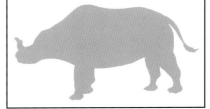

185

MIOCENE

5 mya

10

15

20 mya

OLIGOCENE

25

30

35

EOCENE

40 mya

45

50

PALEOCENE

55

60 mya

65

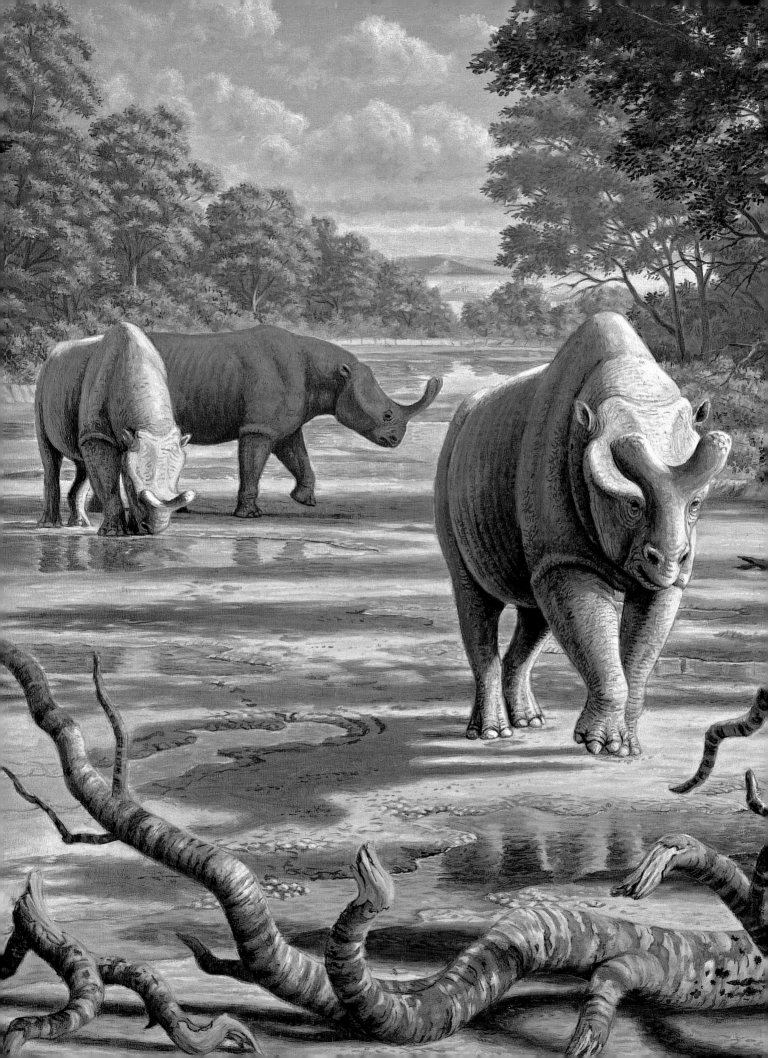

Brontotheres

The tanklike Megacerops, larger than living rhinoceroses, fed on soft forest vegetation. It shared its late Eocene North American habitat with the saber-toothed cat Hoplophoneus.

Museums

Fossil mammals can be seen in a huge number of national and local museums. Here are just a few to aid readers.

Argentina
Bernardino Ribadavia Museum, Buenos Aires; Museo Argentino de Ciancias Naturales, Buenos Aires; Museo de La Plata, La Plata; Museum of La Plata University, La Plata

Australia
Australian Museum, Sydney

Canada
Provincial Museum of Alberta, Edmonton; Royal Ontario Museum, Toronto

China
Institute of Vertebrate Paleontology and Paleoanthropology, Beijing

France
Guimet Museum of Natural History, Lyon; National Museum of Natural History, Paris

Germany
Natural History Museum of Stuttgart; Senckenberg Museum, Frankfurt

Italy
Earth Science Museum, University of Florence

Kenya
National Museums of Kenya, Nairobi

Russia
Paleontological Institute of the National Academy of Sciences, Moscow

South Africa
South African Museum, Cape Town; Transvaal Museum, Pretoria

Spain
Museo Nacional de Ciencias Naturales, Madrid; Instituto de Paleontologia Miquel Crusafont, Sabadell

Sweden
Swedish Museum of Natural History, Stockholm

Switzerland
Natural History Museum, Basel

United Kingdom
Natural History Museum, London; University Museum of Natural History, Oxford

United States
American Museum of Natural History, New York; Carnegie Museum of Natural History, Pittsburgh; Denver Museum of Natural History, Denver; Field Museum of Natural History, Chicago; G.C. Page Museum, Los Angeles; Minnesota Museum of Natural History, Saint Paul; National Museum of Natural History, Washington, D.C.; Museum of Natural History, Yale, New Haven, CT

Glossary of terms

adaptation A characteristic of a living thing that has evolved for a purpose. For example, the square, high-crowned teeth of horses are adapted for eating grass, a very abrasive food.

ancestor An earlier member in the family tree of an animal.

antler A bony structure on the head of deer. Unlike horns, antlers lack the covering of horny keratin that makes the horn sheath.

arboreal Living in trees.

bipedal Moving on the two hind legs.

browsing Eating leaves. Animals such as deer and many antelopes are browsers.

camouflage Coat patterning that blends with the background.

canines Long, pointed teeth at the corners of the jaw. The fangs of lions and dogs are canines.

carnassials Teeth toward the rear of the jaw that carnivores use to slice meat.

carnivores Meat-eating animals.

cetaceans Whales, dolphins, and porpoises.

convergence Similar features, such as the long legs of horses and deer, that appear in unrelated or distantly related animals as a result of evolution to cope with similar environments.

coprolite Preserved dung. Fossilized coprolites date back millions of years, dried and hardened coprolites thousands of years.

cynodonts A group of mammal-like reptiles including the ancestors of true mammals.

deposit Material, including soil, rock, and fossils, that has accumulated at a site.

diaphragm A structure of tough tissue separating the chest (which contains the lungs and heart) from the abdomen (which contains the intestines, or gut). It helps to make breathing easier.

dispersal Movement, often in different directions, of a population or species away from a point or region of origin.

diversity Variation of a group of animals in form and appearance—for example, the bats, with over 1,000 species, are very diverse.

environment The surroundings of an animal or plant.

epoch A division of geological time, such as the Pliocene. A number of epochs make up a period, such as the Tertiary.

era A major division of geological time. Eras consist of periods—for example, the Mesozoic Era consists of the Triassic, Jurassic, and Cretaceous periods.

Eurasia The landmass onsisting of Europe and Asia.

evolution Change in animals or plants over time that results in new species.

extant Of species or groups still living.

extinct Species no longer living.

family The formal group to which related genera belong. For example, the horses belong to the family Equidae, or equids.

fauna The range of all animals found in a particular region or, in the case of fossil animals, a particular time period.

fossil Literally, something dug up. The term is now restricted to remains of formerly living things, with the implication that they have been transformed into hardened and in many cases stonelike objects by minerals in the ground.

fossil record The pattern of past life, with its first appearances and extinctions, that we know from fossils.

genus (plural genera) A group of related species descended from a single common species and belonging to the same family.

gestation The development of the young of any mammal up to the time of birth.

glaciation A period of major ice growth and climatic cooling below the range of normal climates today; another term for an ice age.

grazer An animal that eats mainly grasses. Obvious examples are horses, but many antelopes also prefer grass.

habitat The natural place where an animal or plant lives.

herbivores Animals that eat plants.

hominids The informal name for the family Hominidae. This contains the living great apes—gorilla, chimpanzee, and orangutan—and their immediate fossil relatives, as well as living humans and their fossil relatives.

hominins The informal name for the group, or tribe, Hominini. This is the tribe to which humans and their fossil relatives belong.

hominoids The informal name for the superfamily Hominoidea. This is the group to which humans, living great apes, the gibbons, and several primitive fossil apes belong.

hoof The foot of a plant-eating animal. The term is often applied to the horny material known as keratin, similar to our fingernails, that encases the toes where they meet the ground.

horn A permanent structure, usually long and pointed, on the head of an animal, not to be confused with antlers. In antelopes and their relatives, it consists of a bony interior core and an exterior sheath of keratinized hard tissue, similar to our fingernails. In the case of rhinos, it is made up of highly compressed hair, also made of keratin, and has no interior core. *See also* **keratin.**

ice age A period when large areas of the continents were covered with ice sheets and glaciers. *See also* **glaciation.**

incisors The teeth at the front

of the mouth, used for biting off food.

insectivores Animals that eat mainly insects.

interglacial The period between ice ages, or glaciations. By definition, interglacials are as warm as or warmer than the present day.

keratin The material from which hair, fingernails, hooves, and horn are made.

land bridge Narrow neck of land joining continents or islands, exposed during times of extremely low sea levels or perhaps pushed up by Earth movements.

layer A particular band of deposits in a fossil site.

lineage The ancestral line of a given species.

marsupials The pouched mammals of Australia and the Americas. The young are born in a very undeveloped state and transfer to the pouch, where they grow for some time.

mass extinction An event in the fossil record when a large number of animals and plants appear to have become extinct at the same time.

molars Teeth at the rear of the jaw in mammals. They are commonly used for chewing food in a grinding or crushing manner.

monotremes Mammals that lay eggs.

mya Abbreviation for million years ago.

New World The Americas.

nocturnal Active at night.

Old World Europe and Asia.

omnivores Animals that eat both flesh and plant matter.

order A group of related families. Thus the order

Carnivora includes among others the cat, dog, and bear families.

paleontologist A person who studies fossil plants and animals.

period A division of geological time. Periods, such as the Tertiary, contain epochs, such as the Miocene or Pliocene. Periods are grouped into eras.

perissodactyls Hoofed mammals with an odd number of toes on each foot. The weight is usually taken on the third toe.

placental mammals Mammals whose young develop inside the mother's womb. They are attached by the placenta, through which blood and nutrition are supplied.

plantigrade Walking on the entire foot, or an animal that does so, such as bears and humans.

predator An animal that hunts and captures other creatures for food.

premolars Teeth, lying in front of the molars, that are used for gripping or breaking food. They may also form part of the grinding and crushing function of the molars, depending on the kind of food eaten.

primitive Of a living thing or part of one, at an early stage of evolution. The term is often used loosely to mean "not advanced."

reconstruction Putting together the parts of a fossil animal to show and understand what the living form would have looked like.

ruminants Animals such as cows that regurgitate food to chew slowly while relaxed.

scavengers Animals that actively seek food left over from the kills of others or that has been produced by natural deaths.

sedimentary rocks Rocks that

have formed by the accumulation of material carried by wind or water. They are usually formed of mud, sand, or clay, and often contain fossils.

specialized Describing an animal, or a body part of an animal, that has evolved in a particular way that allows little choice in activity. Pandas specialize in eating bamboo.

species The basic unit of a plant or animal type. In general, species do not breed successfully in the wild with creatures of another species.

stereoscopic vision Seeing objects with both eyes at once. The brain thus gets two slightly different images, and can use this information to judge distance.

teeth, cheek The teeth that typically lie behind the cheeks of an animal. These usually consist of premolars and molars.

teeth, low- or high-crowned The relative height of the part of the tooth that lies above the jaw. High-crowned teeth are typically those that will receive a lot of wear from hard or tough material during the life of the animal.

therapsids An extinct order containing the advanced mammal-like reptiles.

ungulates Animals that walk on the tips of their toes. Modern ungulates are herbivores, such as horses, deer, and antelopes, but some early ungulates were also meat-eaters.

vertebrates Animals with an internal, hard skeleton. All mammals, fish, birds, amphibians, and reptiles are vertebrates.

warm-blooded Of animals that maintain a constant temperature independent of that of their surroundings.

Index

One of the world's largest nonprofit scientific and educational organizations,
the National Geographic Society was founded in 1888 "for the increase and diffusion
of geographic knowledge." Fulfilling this mission, the Society educates and inspires
millions every day through its magazines, books, television programs, videos, maps
and atlases, research grants, the National Geographic Bee, teacher workshops, and
innovative classroom materials.
The Society is supported through membership dues, charitable gifts, and income from
the sale of its educational products. This support is vital to National Geographic's mission to increase global understanding and promote conservation of our planet through
exploration, research, and education.

For more information, please call 1-800-NGS LINE (647-5463) or
write to the following address:

Ｎａｔｉｏｎａｌ Ｇｅｏｇｒａｐｈｉｃ Ｓｏｃｉｅｔｙ
1145 17th Street N.W.
Washington, D.C. 20036-4688 U.S.A.

Visit the Society's Web site at www.nationalgeographic.com.